PV3-18-46747

D1145163

Data Processing Training Handbook

Data Processing Training Handbook

230301

Cost Justification, Measurement, and Evaluation

Gary Slaughter
President, Brandon Systems Institute

QA76,27
S55

PBI
a petrocelli
book
new york / princeton

Copyright © 1979 Petrocelli Books, Inc.

All rights reserved.
Printed in the United States

1 2 3 4 5 6 7 8 9 10

Designed by Joan Greenfield

Library of Congress Cataloging in Publication Data
Slaughter, Gary.
Data processing training handbook.
(PBI series for the computer and data processing professional)
Bibliography: p.
Includes index.
1. Electronic data processing–Study and teaching.
2. Electronic data processing personnel, Training of.
I. Title. II. Series.
QA76.27.S55   658.31'243   79-17795
ISBN 0-89433-118-3

CONTENTS

FOREWORD

Since the early 1970s, DP training has become a more formalized part of the DP organization. Problems of increased personnel costs, turnover, and productivity have focused attention on DP training and have enlarged top management's expectations for results from DP training. Increased costs for training have necessitated more careful shopping, better budgeting and control, and the need for additional justification of expenditures of dollars and of personnel hours on training.

Still, many DP managers and training directors question or, perhaps, ignore the need to justify, measure, and evaluate training. Moreover, because many DP trainers know more about "DP" than "training," they may not know *how* to justify training and *how* to measure and evaluate training to make sure that it continues to deliver its anticipated benefits.

This book addresses the reasons for justifying DP training, how to justify it, and how to measure its effectiveness. Finally, this book assesses the readiness of your DP organization to move ahead with a cost-effective training program by providing a way to analyze the current status of your DP organization compared to other DP organizations already having formal training programs.

Approaches to justify, evaluate, and measure "DP training" are discussed. For purposes of definition, DP training is all training that is presented to people in the DP organization including management, personal improvement, and other training not specifically related to DP subjects.

This book is intended for DP training directors who are responsible for implementing a cost-effective DP training program for their organizations. The secondary audience is DP managers who perform an active role in improving their organization's most valuable resource—its people.

CHAPTER 1

WHY JUSTIFY, MEASURE, AND EVALUATE DP TRAINING?

Justification Defined

As DP professionals, we are known for our obsession with precision. Some of us devote lifetimes to reducing rounding errors to an nth fraction of one percent of a cent, increasing CPU processing times to nanosecond speeds, and cutting program run times by a percent or two. Yet, often, we devote almost no time to being precise in the way that we spend over 70 percent of our DP budgets—on the human resource. Spending for training has been among the least precise of all of our DP people cost expenditures. It's time we ended our imprecision in this area and started justifying, measuring, and evaluating DP training. This chapter will discuss the reasons why.

First, let's define "justify." In the case of DP training, there are two kinds of justification. The first is "cost justification." This is the rarer form of justification; it is seldom found in real life. The second kind is "credibility justification." If you find justification at all, chances are it's some form of credibility justification.

Here are the more precise definitions. *Cost justification* is based on an objective appraisal of the benefits and costs of DP training. *Credibility justification* is based on such elements as the goodwill of top management, the sympathetic cooperation of students, the "acting ability" of instructors, and the public relations acumen of DP training directors. Credibility justification tends to be acceptable in good times and unacceptable in bad times. As everyone knows, credibility is ephemeral.

Credibility justification is, however, absolutely essential. Without it, you have no top management support and no support from your constituents, the students. But, you should not rely on credibility justification alone. Credibility justification should be backed with solid cost justification. Today, more than ever, cost justification of DP training is essential to preserve and promote an effective training program. In addition, an effective program of measurement and evaluation is also required. Here is why.

Solving Management Problems

Properly cost-justified, measured, and evaluated training is more effective training. More effective training can help solve the following problems.

Turnover

In times of economic recession, turnover is not a problem. The economy is sluggish, expenditures on new systems development projects are curtailed, and most people are reluctant to leave their current positions. In prosperous times, quite the opposite is true. The first people to leave are almost always among the most talented. The true cost of turnover is not having the properly qualified person in the position when the job must be done. Having to substitute people and to make do with less than fully competent staff members results in inefficiency, poorly developed systems, and frustration down the road.

During a recent prosperous era that brought on extreme turnover problems, a large New York bank reportedly offered any programmer with two year's experience a flat ten thousand dollar salary increase to work for the bank. DP personnel placement agents were making unheard of commissions. Companies that needed people were offering placement organizations double their normal fee to entice placement agents to look for them. There were charges that certain agents were luring earlier placees away to even higher paying jobs before the placees had spent a year on the job.

A recent study conducted (during a high turnover time in our industry) by a DP training director showed a direct relationship in his organization between turnover and DP training. His study showed that loyalty to his organization was strengthened if DP employees were given the benefit of an active DP training program for their job and career enhancement. Findings of this kind are proper elements of a DP training cost justification and lead directly to enhanced credibility for DP training.

Cost of recruiting and hiring new people

Besides the cost of having no person available to fulfill a vital function when the project demands it, the cost of filling that vacancy can also be substantial. During times of high turnover, with so many jobs available for so few qualified applicants, recruiting efforts must be doubled. Costs for advertising, campus visits, interviewing, placement agency fees, entry-level training, and employee orientation time grow rapidly in many organizations.

If effective DP training can reduce turnover and cut recruiting and hiring costs, these cost savings are proper elements of a DP training cost justification and lead directly to enhanced credibility for DP training.

Sagging productivity

There are numerous theories to explain decreased productivity in DP personnel. Some people believe that our affluent society has brought about a change away from the work ethic that predominated our industry in the early days of the 1950s and 1960s. According to this pessimistic view, people today expect more pay for less work and are less concerned about doing a good job. Supposedly, people are not as loyal to an organization as they once were, because of the ease of finding another, better job if their current organization should displease them. This view may not be the true reason for sagging productivity.

Today, more than ever before, we have the ability to measure people's productivity. Whether we take advantage of this opportunity is another question. Some DP organizations have matured and are spending more time on basic management tools such as project management, performance measurement, and standards enforcement. Some have automated the management of their own operations to some degree. This increased availability of productivity measures coupled with increased people costs has given DP managers a greater potential to measure reduced productivity stemming from whatever source.

Although it may be practically impossible to "prove" (as we shall see in the fourth chapter of this book), effective DP training in the area of structured design and programming is one example of how training can be used to enhance people productivity. Structured design and programming may be shown to reduce program bugs, rerun times, desk-checking time, maintenance, and user-DP communication problems. All of these assumed cost savings are elements of a DP training cost justification and lead directly to increased credibility for such training.

Increased cost of the human resource

The average DP salary has risen dramatically over the past five years. In most categories, it has doubled the inflation rate. Not only are salaries increasing, but, also, as the relative cost of hardware is reduced, the proportion of the DP budget spent on the human resource grows. By the early 1980s, we can expect to see 80 percent or more of the DP budget spent on people. This growth rate places special significance on means of stretching the dollar spent on this resource. The more money spent on people, the more important it is to ensure that the money is spent wisely; and, the more important it is to protect the investment in this resource with a sound plan for human resource improvement.

Increased productivity and professionalism, improved user relations, and better project and general management skills now are recognized as practical necessities for getting more DP for the dollar.

The use of effective DP training in this regard can be directly translated into cost-savings that are a part of DP cost justification and also enhance the credibility of the training.

Changing roles of DP users and top management

DP was once the domain of eccentric mathematics majors and mechanically inclined accountants. DP enjoyed a mystique and forbidding aloofness resulting in open-ended budgets, free-wheeling management, and intimidation of both users and top management. This situation has changed radically in the past few years. Suddenly, top managers are asking tough questions about costs and benefits of DP, and DP users are not as easily snowed as they once were. Users are even insisting on getting their money's worth from DP.

DP departments, more and more, are being held accountable for their costs, levels of service, and their contribution to the overall mission of the organization. This situation presents a meaningful opportunity for DP training. Some DP training organizations are charging users to educate them to meet their roles and responsibilities in the user-DP relationship. The DP training directors are then taking the user training revenues and plowing them back into better DP technical and management training. Some old-timers in DP management hold the belief that "what users don't know, won't hurt them." In reality, if you don't train your users, they will train themselves, so you might as well benefit from the process.

Another area of cost-saving potential for DP training is the area of management and personal growth courses for DP managers and technical people. Five years ago, who would have thought that DP training directors would be selecting, developing, or instructing courses on transactional analysis?

Using training to meet the challenge of the changing role of DP within the overall organization offers a real basis for DP training cost justification. This kind of training offers more credibility justification than any other DP training.

Union problems

More and more DP organizations are becoming unionized. This presents a unique problem for DP managers who have now lost some of their flexibility in dealing with the problems discussed above. Certain additional rules must now be followed that make managing more difficult.

DP training is often a positive force in a union-management relationship. Training offered as an additional fringe benefit to union-represented employees can offer substantial benefits to both management and employees. Union employees receiving the training remain more loyal, increase their productivity, and feel that management is looking out for their best interests making both the employee and management happy.

These benefits can sometimes be translated directly into dollar terms for inclusion in the DP training cost justification. Credibility, as usual, will increase as well.

Cost of DP training

Ironically, one of the problems facing DP management is the cost of training personnel. This cost has increased dramatically over the past few years. Inflationary pressures have something to do with this, but the main reason has been the higher salaries and profits demanded by suppliers of DP training. Once, a consultant could be hired to conduct a training course for the same daily rate as that consultant charged for consulting services. Two things changed this. First, the buyer of these training services became more discriminating and began insisting on professionally developed, fully tested training courses taught by competent instructors. Second, as less skilled trainers left the training profession, the more skilled trainers remaining realized that they possessed a valuable commodity, and they began charging for it.

While it is difficult to find a DP training vendor who won't charge you the going rate for training, it is amazingly easy to find a training vendor who will not deliver the high-quality training that you expect for your money. Quality is still an overriding constraint when selecting a course. Remember, what you want to obtain from training is *value*. Value contains two ingredients, quality and cost.

Proper cost justification, measurement, and evaluation and DP training selection are essential to relieve the worry of DP managers over the high cost of training. After all, if DP managers are to make good use of training to ease the other problems facing them, they must be convinced that they are getting their money's worth. Once convinced, the credibility justification of DP training should follow easily and naturally.

Morale problems

Morale is a difficult subject to address, because it is an intangible and impossible to measure concept. But, the morale of loyal and hardworking employees is a vital concern of all good DP managers. Low morale can mean reduced productivity, higher turnover, increased tardiness and absence, and other personnel problems. Employee morale is a particularly sensitive issue during periods of high turnover. High turnover can cause increased work loads on loyal DP staff members. During these periods, less than fully competent employees receive an inordinate amount of management attention while competent loyal employees are often neglected. Also, during this time new people may come aboard with higher salaries than present staff members. This does not help the morale situation either.

DP training can be useful in reducing tensions and rewarding loyal employees. This, of course, is not the ideal objective for training, but, realistically speaking, training is often used successfully for this purpose. Courses offered in attractive cities away from home are traditional means of getting a deserving employee away for a few days to rub elbows with other DP professionals. In-house training can have the same effect on greater numbers of people in a more cost-effective way. Bringing a training professional to your offices tells your people that you think enough of them and their job enrichment to provide them with the very best. Training works to buy loyalty and build morale, thus reducing turnover and saving the DP organization money.

Using effective, cost-justified, measured, and evaluated DP training to avoid the high costs of low morale is an important part of DP training cost justification and enhances the credibility of DP training.

Protecting the DP Training Program

In 1971 and again in 1975, DP training activities decreased drastically. Why? Because most DP training directors had not learned to cost justify their DP training. They were lulled into the false sense of security that reliance on credibility justification often brings. When the euphoria ended abruptly, many DP training directors found themselves out of a job or, at least, given a different assignment. Unfortunately their organization's need for DP training did not subside, only the DP training directors' ability to convince DP management to continue the DP training program subsided. In many cases, with DP budgets for hiring outside consultants and new people cut drastically, the best solution to operating pressures was to have better trained people. However, in most organizations, DP training programs that had just been implemented were abruptly curtailed before they could succeed. For many organizations, it has taken years to regain the momentum that was lost during these two economic downturns.

When preparing to protect your DP training program, there are certain realities about DP training to keep in mind.

DP training is an overhead function

To most cost-cutting controllers, training is another overhead function, lumped together with other expendables like travel, office picnics, and consultant fees. Come the crunch, all these must go.

If this sounds like a gloomy prognosis, keep in mind that training is not just another overhead function in many industries. At budget time in some industries, training, because of proper cost justification, is treated as a sacred cow. For example, a recent study shows that CPA firms plow back 10 percent of their gross revenues into continuing education for their people. What about the airlines? Have you ever heard of a pilot not getting constant refresher and recertification training? And the military? And doctors and nurses? Why not DP? DP training will remain just another overhead function for as long as we are relutant to cost justify expenditures for it.

DP training is deferable

DP training is often the victim of the great "put off." The well-laid plans of many DP training directors are dashed by lack of planning or sensitivity or both by some DP managers, their administrative assistants, students themselves, or, very often, the students' supervisors.

Whenever training is deferred, the organization and the student must pay for it in some way. Training (like any other benefit) deferred is often benefit lost. Remember the adage, you pay for training whether you conduct it or not. You pay for it in tasks improperly completed, low morale, or turnover ... but you pay for it.

The only bright spot in the deferred training situation is that the training opportunity may not be permanently lost. But, training administered without planning and order is likely to be an ineffective program.

DP training takes people away

Whether we like it or not, DP training does cost the students' organization something. For each day of training, you have one day of lost production time. This reality should always temper our thinking about training. We should keep in mind that the greatest cost of training students is their time away from the job. At a minimum, this time should be measured in terms of their fully loaded salary or wage.

This time away from the job is often the cause for cancelled or deferred training. How many people do you know in your DP organization who are so good that they never get an opportunity for training? On the other hand, do you know people who are not in the greatest demand for project team assignments and, thus, end up going to twice as many courses as other people?

Cost justification of DP training can point out these inequities and can help DP managers see the benefits of letting even their best people attend much needed training courses.

Training is a threat to mediocre managers...
and vice versa

Unfortunately, every organization has DP supervisors who, because of ego problems, do not want their subordinates trained. Smart students are a threat to them. These DP supervisors are those people who can no longer compete with their subordinates on the basis of technical competence. But, often they have more to add to the organization in experience, judgment, wisdom, and ability to deal with top management or users than they realize. We have all seen these people who are obviously threatened by a young DP professional who can run technical circles around them.

If you have one of these people in your organization, keep one thing in mind—you are a threat too. If smart students make them uncomfortable, then smart DP training directors are downright unbearable. Solid cost justification is the only approach to breaking down resistance to training. In most cases, solid dollars-and-cents cost savings figures will sway anyone with a modicum of business acumen. If this does not work, escalate your problem to the next level of management for a ruling.

Professionalism and Credibility

If you cannot accept the need for DP training cost justification, measurement, and evaluation because it helps solve some tough problems or because it might save your job, then do it just for the pride of it. It won't be easy, but you won't be sorry.

What if no one else does it?

A recent study reported that only 30 percent of DP organizations are evaluated by top management on the basis of quantified measures of criteria of performance. The same study reported that only 24 percent of DP organizations have quantified the return on their DP investment. Despite the lack of good procedures in the rest of DP, you should still cost justify DP training for two reasons. First, you are a DP trainer, so you're supposed to know more than other people in your organization (that is, do it because you are smarter). Second, do it because, as a DP trainer, you should be setting a good example (that is, do it to make yourself look good).

Why not do it for professionalism?

DP trainers often know more about "DP" than about "training," so why not act as professional in a training sense as you do in a DP sense? After all, according to a recent Hope Report,* the training industry is at least a $20 billion industry. That's about four times as big as the DP industry. Who knows which industry you will end up in? Many DP trainers migrate out of DP into training and human resource development

---

*Single copies of this Hope Report (Vol. 3, No. 1) are available for $10 each from Hope Reports, Inc., 919 S. Winton Road, Rochester, N.Y. 14618.

organizations serving all kinds of people including DP people. Forty-three percent of this country's adults are engaged in some form of adult learning program, and over half of them are engaged in some job-related learning program. You are a part of an important profession when you are a trainer.

Regardless of your reason for doing it, the diligent following of cost-justification procedures will lead to increased credibility with DP managers and your constituents, your students.

Cost Justification, Measurement, and Evaluation Assumptions

If you are now convinced that you should cost justify, measure, and evaluate your DP training, you may be ready to move ahead, provided certain assumptions are true of your situation. These are vital assumptions that can make your cost justification efforts either meaningful or a sham.

Training is the solution to the problem

To some this may seem to be a trivial concern, but it should be taken very seriously if you are to have a bonafide, cost-justified training program. Martin Broadwell,* speaking before a group of DP training directors recently, put it this way: "If the employees couldn't do the job if their life depended on it, then training probably is the only solution. If they can do the job, training may not be the answer at all."

We all know of instances when training is used for the wrong reasons. Use of training as a reward was discussed in the previous section of this chapter. Training is a morale

---

*Martin M. Broadwell, well-known author, lecturer, and consultant in the field of training and human resource development, is the president of Resources for Education and Management, Inc., headquartered in Decatur, Georgia.

builder. Training is sometimes a pigeonhole ... a convenient place to tuck someone away between assignments.

When training is thought of as the only solution to a performance problem, challenge the assumption. Maybe somebody is ducking a responsibility. It could be DP management or maybe you haven't spotted the real problem.

How many organizations have trained people in the use of structured design and programming before thoroughly evaluating the approach's applicability to, and acceptance in, their environment? How many organizations have trained people in structured design and programming without first identifying which of the many structured techniques their organization would use? How many organizations did this training without first obtaining the full support of all supervisors who subsequently resisted the change enough to kill the use of the structured approach in their section?

Does this sound familiar? These problems frequently occur in the area of project management and data base management. Is training the real solution to the problem facing your organization or is it just a convenient rationalization to duck the real issue? Or worse yet, is training the scapegoat for insufficient homework and decision making?

Be sure that training is the solution to the problem before trying to cost justify, measure, and evaluate training. If you do not, the failure of the training could mean the failure of your justification approach and the complete destruction of your stock of credibility.

Identify the right training solution

The best way to be sure that the training solution that you have identified is the right training solution is to conduct a task analysis for your organization. After completion of task analysis, conduct a skills analysis. Upon comparison, you can identify training deficiencies and training course objectives can be set. Next, you must compare your selected course's training objectives with those objectives that you have identified as needed. If they match, you have selected the right training course. If they do not match, further searching or development of your own course might be indicated.*

Establish course evaluation criteria first

Before you can say with certainty that a selected training course is right, you must identify standards of performance for each task identified in your task analysis. For example, it is not enough to identify a training course objective as, "Upon successful completion of this course, the student will be able to code program statements in COBOL." Almost any COBOL training course could guarantee meeting that objective. You should establish performance standards to accompany each task and, thus, each training objective. As a simple example, you might establish a training course objective that reads, "Upon successful completion of this course, the student will be able to code an average of 25 program statements in COBOL per hour."

This insistence on established evaluation criteria will become much more important after the course presentation when you are attempting to measure and evaluate the success of the course. The upcoming chapter dealing with measurement and evaluation will present more information on this subject.

Summary

This chapter has discussed the reasons for cost justifying DP training. Proper cost-justified, measured, and evaluated DP training is effective DP training. Effective training is a valu-

---

*BSI presents a five-day course, *How to Implement a DP Human Resource Development Program* (HRD), which teaches DP training directors to conduct task and skills analysis and to set training course objectives.

able tool in helping DP management face the tough problems related to obtaining maximum return on investment in the human resource. Cost justification, measurement, and evaluation can be used simply to preserve and protect the training organization within DP. Organizations which do not follow these three procedures often lose their training programs when an economic downturn occurs. DP trainers may want to cost justify, measure, and evaluate DP training simply to enhance their professionalism and credibility with their organization. Cost justification, measurement, and evaluation will work when the right solution to the performance problem has been identified and agreed-upon evaluation criteria are established *before* the course is conducted.

CHAPTER 2

HOW TO COST JUSTIFY DP TRAINING

Management Education Requirements

Before you can benefit from DP training cost justification, top DP management must be "educated" to appreciate the products of your cost justification efforts. Before educating DP management, educate yourself to ensure that you know what method of cost justification to use under what circumstances and how to apply that method properly.

The first step in your education process is to understand the terms associated with cost justification. What do we mean by "cost"? Cost may be measured in either economic or noneconomic terms. "Economic costs" for training include items such as teaching and development costs, student salaries, and overhead. "Noneconomic costs" cover such things as loss of productivity or reduced morale. Most noneconomic costs can ultimately be translated into economic costs, but they are intangible and require a degree of assumption and judgment to assign economic values to them. This is what must be done in cost-effectiveness analysis discussed later in this chapter. Some people prefer to think of economic costs as "tangible costs" and noneconomic costs as "intangible costs." Unfortunately, many decision makers confuse the term "cost" with "cost-benefit" or "cost-effective." They feel that the most effective form of DP training is that which costs the least. This is the primary reason to educate DP management and others who control or influence the DP training budget.

What are "cost-benefit" and "cost-effectiveness" analyses? "Cost-benefit" analysis is the evaluation of alternative means to achieve a given objective when the value of the objective and the costs associated with achieving it are stated in economic terms. "Cost-effectiveness analysis" is the evaluation of alternative means to achieve a given objective when the value of the objective and the costs associated with achieving it are stated in noneconomic as well as economic terms. Cost justification of DP training is usually best achieved by using cost-effectiveness analysis.

Regardless of the cost-justification approach used, the objectives of a DP training program should be stated in terms of conventional learning objectives *and* in terms of economic or financial objectives. DP and top management must be educated to think of DP training as an investment that will pay off, according to a preplanned set of objectives, over a period of time in the future. No one likes to spend money, but everyone likes to invest wisely.

Cost-Justification Approaches

There are two quantitative cost-justification approaches that are useful to the DP training director. These approaches may be characterized as "hard" and "soft" approaches. Proper use of either approach depends on the circumstances.

"Hard" cost justification

Hard justification approaches are best used under three conditions:

1. *Available time and importance.* Under this circumstance you have enough time to do a thorough job, and the job is worth doing. This assumes that the course or program under consideration is being planned deliberately and will be conducted for enough students in the organization to make it worth the effort to justify using a hard justification approach.

2. *Large training investment.* You have a large enough potential dollar investment in the proposed training to invest significant time and money in its justification.

3. *Available data to conduct justification.* If you are to use a hard cost-justification approach, you must have the economic data required to do so. You also need the support and involvement of management to assist you in assigning values to costs and benefits which have not yet been quantified.

"Soft" cost justification

Soft justification approaches are also used under three conditions:

1. *Short fuse.* This means you do not have enough time to do a thorough job, because operational necessity dictates that you move ahead rapidly with the training. Regardless of the time (or lack of it) available, the justification must be done to give DP management the cost-conscious overview that is required to maintain your credibility as DP training director. Surprisingly, a quick cost justification will sometimes reverse what would have been an unwise, impulsive training decision.

2. *Small dollar items*. When few dollars are involved, an elaborate cost-justification method is not required. Small training transactions may be lumped together and justified as an overall program; for example, a number of vendor public courses for systems programmers may be approved as a group, then a simple administration justification methodology may be established to approve each public course as that course is required by each systems programmer.

3. *Insufficient data*. There may be time to justify a rather large-dollar training program, but there may not be enough data to do an effective cost-justification job. There may be indecision or disagreement among DP or user people as to the value that should be assigned to noneconomic benefits or costs. Occasionally, the benefit is not significant or, at least, not readily apparent, but the training must be done anyway, e.g., training ordered by top corporate management for all corporate employees or training required to comply with a recently passed law. When you do not have sufficient data to cost justify DP training, simply admit it to DP management. Inadequate cost justifications will reflect poorly on you.

Hard Cost-justification Approaches

Cost effectiveness analysis

AN OVERVIEW. Cost-effectiveness analysis of DP training involves the evaluation of alternative means to achieve a DP department operational objective (usually meeting a user department need). The costs and benefits of these alternatives must be compared to the costs and benefits of the status quo.

In some cases, the result of cost-effectiveness analysis is to conclude that no reasonable alternative to the status quo is cost effective, and, thus, "no action" is the recommended solution. Realistically, alternative means of achieving a DP department objective may include choices other than training. For example, if the DP department faces a difficult conversion from a no-data-base-system environment to IMS, department management could hire experienced IMS people *or* could train DP department personnel in IMS skills *or* could bring in IMS consultants to do the conversion. All three choices are potential solutions to what, at first, might appear to be a DP training problem. Therefore, cost-effectiveness analysis must look at the cost and benefits of the status quo, the nontraining solutions, and the alternative training solutions.

When conducting a DP cost-effectiveness analysis, remember that you must take into account *noneconomic* or *intangible costs* and *benefits*. Benefits are usually the elimination of all or some costs associated with the status quo; they are in effect negative costs. Many DP training cost-effectiveness analyses are, in reality, only a comparison of the economic or tangible costs of the available DP training alternatives. Identifying economic costs of DP training is extremely important, but it is only part of the job. Remember the adage, "We always calculate the cost of doing training—but seldom the cost of not doing it." Good cost-effectiveness analysis does both.

A proper cost-effectiveness analysis will include all economic and noneconomic costs in the following categories:

Training staff costs

Student costs

Facilities costs

Vendor costs

Operational effectiveness or organizational costs

A proper cost-effectiveness analysis will also include all economic and noneconomic benefits in the following categories:

Operational effectiveness or organizational benefits

Student benefits

Training staff benefits

Exhibit 2.1 is a comprehensive *Cost and Benefit Check List* showing the detailed breakdown of above cost and benefit categories for the three common DP training alternatives: (1)

Exhibit 2.1: Cost and Benefit Check List _____

This check list should be used for preparing cost-effectiveness analyses by identifying all costs and benefits associated with the three common DP training alternatives: (1) self-developed and presented training; (2) vendor in-house training; and (3) vendor public training.

PART I. SELF-DEVELOPED AND PRESENTED TRAINING

The training solution to the operational problem is designed, developed, and taught by DP training staff personnel with the assistance of user personnel and other DP department personnel.

1. Costs (and Time)

A. DP TRAINING STAFF COSTS. (All expenditures for DP training staff members' time will be expressed in dollars representing the average salary and overhead for the DP training group.)

1. How much time will be spent in conducting research prior to the start of course development?
2. What will be the cost for technical and professional books, films, periodicals, and other materials necessary to build a library on the course subject? How much staff time will be spent gathering and reviewing these materials?
3. Will the staff review and evaluate the public presentation of courses on this subject offered by various vendors? If so, how much time will be spent in doing so?
4. Will it be necessary for staff members to travel to user sites or to other

self-developed and presented training; (2) vendor in-house training; and (3) vendor public training.

Exhibit 2.2 is a simplified *Cost-Effectiveness Analysis Example* of the status quo, reasonable nontraining alternatives, and the three common training alternatives for an apparent systems analysis training solution to a DP department operational problem. The *Cost and Benefit Check List* in Exhibit 2.1 was used to derive detailed dollar figures for the various alternatives.

DP department locations to complete the course development? If so, how much will be spent for travel and subsistence and DP training staff time? How much time will user or DP department personnel spend at the site visited?

5. Once the course is developed, tested, and accepted for general use, how much course-maintenance time will be required from the DP training staff? During the first year of training? In subsequent years?

6. Will consultants be used in course design or development? How much will be required for consultant fees? Travel and subsistence?

7. How much will be spent on course materials including artwork, typing, visuals, printing, notebooks, films, special equipment, computer time for testing course exercises, and other supplies? Initially? For subsequent offerings of the course?

8. How much time will be required to develop and to test the course? How much time for training of the trainers?

9. How much time will be spent on teaching the course? First year? Future years? What will travel and subsistence cost?

10. How much time will be spent on coordinating and administering student registrations?

11. How much time will be spent on cost justification prior to the commitment to the course development project?

12. How much time will be spent on course evaluation?

B. STUDENT COSTS.

(All expenditures for students' time will be expressed in dollars representing the average salary and overhead for the student group.)

Exhibit 2.1 (continued) ───────────────────────────────

1. Will students be involved in course development as consultants to the development project? As reviewers or sources of information during course development? What will be the cost in time? Travel and subsistence?
2. During the test and subsequent presentations, how many students will be attending the course? What will the ultimate course length be? How much student time will be involved with course attendance? With travel to and from the course?
3. What will be the cost per student of course materials and supplies, refreshments, and other course conduct costs?

C. FACILITIES COSTS.

(Facilities costs include rent, maintenance, janitorial services, utilities, and a standard overhead allocation.)

1. What will be the cost of using special facilities and equipment during course development?
2. What is the cost of classroom space and equipment for the test course? For subsequent courses?
3. Does the new course indicate the need for renovation, remodeling, or new construction of training space? At what cost?
4. Will a computer be required to develop or teach the course? If so, at what cost?
5. Will there be a requirement for off-site facilities? What are costs for hotel meeting rooms? Audio-visual equipment rentals? Course material delivery expenses? Computer terminal charges?
6. What proportion of the annual DP training staff yearly budget for office space will be absorbed in the direct support of this course?
7. If new training staff members are required to develop or teach this course, how much added office space and equipment is needed? Cost?

D. VENDOR COSTS

1. Will it be necessary to purchase vendor materials, textbooks, films, audio-visual aids, or other materials? If so, at what cost initially? For subsequent courses?
2. Will the use of vendor materials require payment of a royalty to the vendor?

E. OPERATIONAL EFFECTIVENESS OR
ORGANIZATIONAL COSTS

1. Will there be any economic impact on the DP department or organization as a whole caused by the development and subsequent presentations of this course? If so, what will it cost?
2. Will DP or other organization personnel be required to assist in the development or teaching of this course? At what cost?

2. Benefits

(Benefits are usually costs that will be eliminated by training. Benefits are, in effect, negative costs.)

A. OPERATIONAL EFFECTIVENESS OR
ORGANIZATIONAL BENEFITS

1. How will this training reduce the use of people's time in the process being addressed or affected by this training course? In the DP department? In the organization as a whole?
2. How will staffing levels be affected if the student successfully performs the skills taught by this course? In the DP department? In the organization as a whole?
3. How much equipment cost savings will be realized if the students successfully perform the skills taught by this course? In the DP department? In the organization as a whole?
4. How will successful completion of this course improve service provided to customers, users, or top management? What is this improved service worth? In the DP department? In the organization as a whole?
5. How will successful completion of this training course reduce missed deadlines for DP department production or project activities? How much savings will be realized?
6. How much savings would result from improved quality work from students who successfully complete this training? In the DP department? In the organization as a whole?
7. How much savings would result from improved productivity of students who successfully complete this course? In the DP department? In the organization as a whole?

Exhibit 2.1 (continued) —————————————————————————

8. How much value would result from a course built around a case study developed from a real operation in the DP department or another part of the organization? Value to the DP department? Value to the organization as a whole?

B. STUDENT BENEFITS

1. Will this course reduce turnover in the student group? How much cost would be associated with this turnover in terms of recruiting costs, placement fees, new employee orientation time, lost on-the-job availability, and so on?

2. How will increased professionalism of the student group affect the overall performance of the DP department? The organization as a whole? What value should be assigned to this improved professionalism?

3. How will this course improve the students' ability to advance to higher levels in the organization, thus making them more valuable?

4. How much will this course improve the organization's ability to recruit superior people (inside or outside) by increasing the company loyalty of the students, thus increasing their influence as recruiters?

C. DP TRAINING STAFF BENEFITS

1. How much will undertaking this new course development project reduce turnover of the DP training staff? How much cost would be associated with this turnover in terms of recruiting costs, placement fees, new employee orientation time, lost teaching resources, and so on?

2. How will increased professionalism of the DP training staff affect the overall performance of the DP department?

3. What residual or transferable benefit will this course have when it is time to develop a new version of it? When it is time to develop a related course?

Part II. VENDOR IN-HOUSE TRAINING

This training solution to the operational problem is to contract with a training vendor to bring that vendor's course of instruction to your offices for presentation to a number of people in your own facilities.

1. Costs (and Time)

A. DP TRAINING STAFF COSTS. (All expenditures for DP training staff members' time will be expressed in dollars representing the average salary and overhead for the DP training group.)

1. How much time will be spent on conducting research on the course subject before selection of the in-house training vendor?
2. Will the DP training staff review the vendor's public offering of the course prior to selecting the in-house training vendor? How much will be spent on staff travel and living? Course fees? Other materials?
3. How much staff time will be spent on reviewing and evaluating vendor courses?
4. How much staff time will be spent on vendor negotiations, course coordination, and follow-up?
5. Will the staff sit through the vendor-presented course? The first time? Subsequent times? How much time will be involved in quality control of the in-house vendor's course presentations?
6. How much staff time will be spent on coordinating and administering student registrations?
7. How much staff time will be spent on cost justification prior to selection of the in-house vendor?
8. How much staff time will be spent on course evaluation?

B. STUDENT COSTS.

(All expenditures for students' time will be expressed in dollars representing the average salary and overhead for the student group.)

1. Will students be involved in in-house course selection as consultants to the course selection project? What will be the cost in time? Travel and subsistence?
2. How much student time will be involved with course attendance? Subsistence and travel to and from the course?
3. What will be the cost per student of materials and supplies, refreshments, and other course conduct costs?

C. FACILITIES COSTS

1. What is the cost of classroom space and equipment for the presentation of the in-house vendor course?

Exhibit 2.1 *(continued)* _____

2. Does the new course indicate the need for renovation, remodeling, or new construction of training space? At what cost?
3. Will a computer be required to teach this course? If so, at what cost?
4. Will there be a requirement for off-site facilities? What are the costs for hotel meeting rooms? Audio-visual equipment rentals? Student refreshments and meals? Course material delivery expenses? Computer terminal charges?

D. VENDOR COSTS

1. How much is the in-house course basic fee? How many students does it cover? Are there additional student fees for students over a fixed number?
2. How much are vendor travel and subsistence and course material delivery charges?
3. Will you require the vendor to make an on-site visit to your offices prior to presentation of the course? Vendor fee? Travel and subsistence?
4. Will you require the vendor to tailor the vendor's standard, off-the-shelf course for you prior to presentation? What will be the cost? Incidentally, who will own the course if it is tailored to your needs?

E. OPERATIONAL EFFECTIVENESS OR
ORGANIZATIONAL COSTS

1. Will there be any economic impact on the DP department or organization as a whole caused by vendor in-house presentation of this course? If so, what will it cost?
2. Will DP department or other organizational personnel be required to assist in the selection of this in-house vendor course? At what cost?

2. Benefits

(Benefits are usually costs that will be eliminated by training. Benefits are, in effect, negative costs.)

A. OPERATIONAL EFFECTIVENESS OR
ORGANIZATIONAL BENEFITS

1. How will this training reduce the use of people's time in the process being addressed or affected by this training course? In the DP department? In the organization as a whole?

2. How will staffing levels be affected if the student successfully performs the skills taught by this course? In the DP department? In the organization as a whole?
3. How much equipment cost savings will be realized if the students successfully perform the skills taught by this course? In the DP department? In the organization as a whole?
4. How will successful completion of this course improve service provided to customers, users, or top management? What is this improved service worth? In the DP department? In the organization as a whole?
5. How will successful completion of this training course reduce missed deadlines for DP department production or project activities? How much savings will be realized?
6. How much savings would result from improved quality work from students who successfully complete this training? In the DP department? In the organization as a whole?
7. How much savings would result from improved productivity of students who successfully complete this course? In the DP department? In the organization as a whole?

B. STUDENT BENEFITS

1. Will this course reduce turnover in the student group? How much cost would be associated with this turnover in terms of recruiting costs, placement fees, new employee orientation time, lost on-the-job availability, and so on?
2. How will increased professionalism of the student group affect the overall performance of the DP department? The organization as a whole? What value should be assigned to this improved professionalism?
3. How will this course improve the students' ability to advance to higher levels in the organization, thus making them more valuable?
4. How much will this course improve the organization's ability to recruit superior people (inside or outside) by increasing the company loyalty of the students, thus increasing their influence as recruiters?

C. DP TRAINING STAFF BENEFITS

1. How much will the researching, selecting, and negotiating involved in the presentation of this course reduce turnover of the DP training

Exhibit 2.1 (continued) _____

staff? How much cost would be associated with this turnover in terms of recruiting costs, placement fees, new employee orientation time, lost teaching resources, and so on?

2. What is the value of having the DP training staff available for other course development and presentation activities now that a vendor will teach this course?

PART III. VENDOR PUBLIC TRAINING

This training solution to the operational problem is to enroll your organization's students in a vendor's public offerings of the course of instruction.

1. Costs (and Time)

A. DP TRAINING STAFF COSTS. (All expenditures for DP training staff members' time will be expressed in dollars representing the average salary and overhead for the DP training group.)

1. How much time will be spent on researching the course subject before selection of the public training vendor?
2. Will the staff review the public course prior to selecting the public training vendor? How much time will be spent on reviewing and selecting the right course? How much time will be spent on staff travel and living? Course fees? Other materials?
3. How much staff time will be spent on coordinating and administering student registrations?
4. How much staff time will be spent on cost justification prior to selection of the public training alternative?
5. How much staff time will be spent on course evaluation?

B. STUDENT COSTS. (All expenditures for students' time will be expressed in dollars representing the average salary and overhead for the student group.)

1. Will students be involved with the selection of the public training vendor course? What will be the cost in time? Travel and subsistence?
2. How much student time will be involved with course attendance? Travel to and from the course? What about travel and subsistence while out of the office?

C. FACILITIES COSTS

1. Will there be any increase in staff office needs to support this training program? How much will it cost?

D. VENDOR COSTS

1. What is the cost for student course registration fees? For course material?

E. OPERATIONAL EFFECTIVENESS OR
ORGANIZATIONAL COSTS

1. Will there be any economic impact on the DP department or organization as a whole caused by vendor public presentation of this course? If so, what will it cost?
2. Will DP department or other organization personnel be required to assist in the selection of this public vendor course? At what cost?
3. Is having students out of town and therefore out of reach of the DP department in case of an emergency costly? If so, how costly?

2. Benefits

(Benefits are usually costs that will be eliminated by training. Benefits are, in effect, negative costs.)

A. OPERATIONAL EFFECTIVENESS OR ORGANIZATIONAL BENEFITS

1. How will this training reduce the use of people's time in the process being addressed or affected by this training course? In the DP department? In the organization as a whole?
2. How will staffing levels be affected if the student successfully performs the skills taught by this course? In the DP department? In the organization as a whole?
3. How much equipment cost savings will be realized if the students successfully perform the skills taught by this course? In the DP department? In the organization as a whole?
4. How will successful completion of this course improve service provided to customers, users, or top management? What is this improved service worth? In the DP department? In the organization as a whole?

Exhibit 2.1 (continued) _____

5. How will successful completion of this training course reduce missed deadlines for DP department production or project activities? How much savings will be realized?
6. How much savings would result from improved quality work from students who successfully complete this course? In the DP department? In the organization as a whole?
7. How much savings would result from improved productivity of students who successfully complete this course? In the DP department? In the organization as a whole?
8. How much value would result from having students gone from the organization a few at a time in a pattern of flexible scheduling as opposed to having an entire class gone at the same time? Value to DP department? To the organization as a whole?

B. STUDENT BENEFITS

1. Will this course reduce turnover in the student group? How much cost would be associated with this turnover in terms of recruiting costs, placement fees, new employee orientation time, lost on-the-job availability, and so on?

_____

Exhibit 2.2: Cost-Effectiveness Analysis Example _____
Cost justification of a systems analysis workshop.

BACKGROUND

The Owosso Ball Bearing Company (OBB) is a $800 million manufacturing company in the Midwest. OBB top management decided to design and install a major new system for on-line order entry, inventory control, and production control.

The new system is expected to encompass virtually all of the company's nationwide operations and affect all of the company's employees from sales representatives in the field to supervisors in the manufacturing plants who make production decisions relating to filling special orders from OBB's customers. Extensive use of terminals will characterize the new system.

The company presently uses computers principally for accounting

2. How will increased professionalism of the student group affect the overall performance of the DP department? The organization as a whole? What value should be assigned to this improved professionalism?
3. How will this course improve the students' ability to advance to higher levels in the organization, thus making them more valuable?
4. How much will this course improve the organization's ability to recruit superior people (inside or outside) by increasing the company loyalty of the students, thus increasing their influence as recruiters?

C. DP TRAINING STAFF BENEFITS

1. How much will the researching, selecting, and negotiation involved in the presentation of this course reduce turnover of the DP training staff? How much cost would be associated with this turnover in terms of recruiting costs, placement fees, new employee orientation time, lost teaching resources, and so on?
2. What is the value of having the DP training staff available for other course development and presentation activities now that a vendor will teach this course?

---

and payroll purposes. Order entry, inventory control, and production control are manual systems that have been in place for generations. In each key sales office, warehouse, and manufacturing plant, there is a core of old-timers who know precisely how the manual system works and how to use it to make OBB one of the most profitable bearing companies in the world.

OBB top management believes that on-line automation and integration of these complex manual systems will result in significant cost reduction for OBB. The success of the project is critically important to the company. OBB must stay competitive in world markets against stiff competition from German and Japanese ball bearing companies. All eyes are on the DP department.

Exhibit 2.2 (continued) _____

THE DP DEPARTMENT'S CHOICES

The DP department is primed for this new project. Over the past two years the DP manager has worked closely with top corporate management to bring the systems and programming staff up to full manning level in preparation for this extensive multiyear development effort. New employees have been selected for their backgrounds in on-line systems design and programming.

All systems and programming people have attended several weeks of the latest training on the technical aspects of on-line system design and programming using the hardware vendor's equipment. The DP department is competent and ready to go ... technically.

The one big problem is conducting a thorough and effective analysis of the existing manual system to ensure top corporate management that the on-line systems solution that will be developed, designed, and implemented is the right solution to the problem and that this system solution will not only meet all the financial objectives of top corporate management, but also will be accepted by the end-users who currently cherish their manual systems.

To accomplish this important systems analysis function, the DP manager has selected 25 top-notch systems designers and senior programmers to be trained in systems analysis. These new systems analysts will conduct an extensive systems survey and detailed systems analysis before moving to the systems design and implementation phases.

The DP training director recognized the need for systems analysis training and has submitted a preliminary recommendation to the DP manager. Because of the size and importance of the training project, the DP training director has recommended completion of a thorough, hard-cost justification prior to commitment to the systems analysis training.

The DP training director recommends consideration of five alternatives for accomplishing the DP organizational objective of conducting the systems survey and the detailed analysis of the new system. These alternatives are:

1. Status quo, i.e., not training the 25 people at all, but allowing them to tackle the systems analysis job without training.
2. Use of outside systems development consultants to conduct the

systems survey and detailed analysis phases of the systems development project.
3. Conducting systems analysis training in one of three ways:
   A. Self-developed and presented training
   B. Vendor in-house training
   C. Vendor public training

The DP manager agrees with the DP training director and requests a complete cost-effectiveness analysis of these alternatives.

THE COST-EFFECTIVENESS ANALYSIS ITSELF

[The following cost-effectiveness analysis is presented to illustrate the approach used by the DP training director. The data has been summarized for easy understanding. Some methods commonly used in cost-effectiveness analysis were not used in this example, including: (1) inclusion of the present value of future years' benefits by calculating the discounted cash value; and (2) calculation of a range or probabilities of benefit values to give a more realistic view of benefit values.]

Alternative 1: Status Quo

This alternative would have the 25 systems analysts undertake the systems survey and detailed systems analysis phases without systems analysis training.

At best, the systems analysis teams would accomplish these phases, and the resultant system would meet all the financial objectives of top management. At worst, the team would produce the wrong or incomplete systems solution to the business problem, and the system after implementation would not be accepted and would have to be abandoned. The improper conduct of these phases might also result in complete alienation of the end-users causing other operational problems.

For purposes of calculating the costs and benefits associated with this alternative, we have assumed that the use of improperly trained systems analysts to conduct the systems survey phase and detailed systems analysis phase will result in the implementation of a systems solution that will deliver only 90 percent of the potential benefits. We also

Exhibit 2.2 *(continued)* _____

assume there will be a number of disgruntled sales, warehouse, and plant personnel.

CALCULATION OF THE STATUS QUO
COSTS AND BENEFITS

I. COSTS

    A. Nondelivery of potential cost savings (10 percent of $8 million first-year savings) $800,000

    B. Turnover of sales, warehouse, and plant personnel (15 employees @ $5000)   75,000

    C. Turnover of systems analysts (3 @ $5000)   15,000

    D. Management time spent in explaining A–C (35 days @ $150)   5,250

                                   Total cost $895,250

II. BENEFITS

    A. Elimination of systems analysis training costs (assume vendor in-house training is chosen alternative)

                             Total benefits $26,175

                                   Net cost $896,075

Alternative 2: Use of Outside Systems Development Consultants

This alternative would provide for the use of contract systems analysts to conduct the systems survey and detailed systems analysis phase of the systems development project and then turn the project over to OBB systems and programming staff for detailed systems design and implementation.

CALCULATION OF OUTSIDE SYSTEMS
DEVELOPMENT CONSULTANTS COSTS
AND BENEFITS

I. COSTS

    A. Daily consulting rates for systems analysis (1500 days @ $500) $750,000

B. Consultant travel and subsistence (250 site visits
   @ $150)   37,500
C. Turnover of systems analysis (3 @ $5000)   15,000
D. Management time spent on negotiation and ad-
   ministering consulting contract (200 @ $150)   30,000
                                         Total costs $832,500

II. BENEFITS

A. Elimination of systems analysis training costs (assume vendor in-house training is the chosen
   alternative) $ 26,175
B. Elimination of OBB systems analysts' time for conducting systems survey and detailed systems
   analysis phases (1500 @ $125)   187,500
C. Elimination of OBB systems analysts' travel and
   subsistence (250 site visits @ $150)   37,500
D. Delivery of potential cost savings over status quo
   (10 percent of $8 million first-year savings)   800,000
                                      Total benefits $1,051,175
                                        Net benefits $ 218,675

Alternative 3A: Self-developed and Presented Training

This alternative assumes that the DP training staff will develop a high
quality systems analysis workshop using a case study based on the
existing inventory control system. The course will be five days in length
and will be conducted at the OBB home office.

CALCULATION OF SELF-DEVELOPED
AND PRESENTED TRAINING COSTS
AND BENEFITS

I. COSTS

A. DP training staff time conducting research (20
   days @ $125) $ 2,500
B. Technical books and publications   500
C. Public course review (5 days) (fee, travel and subsistence, and time)   1,825

Exhibit 2.2 (continued) ⎯⎯⎯⎯⎯⎯⎯⎯⎯⎯⎯⎯⎯⎯⎯⎯⎯⎯⎯⎯⎯⎯

D. Course development project trips to user sites (3 @ $1,200 including time and travel and subsistence)	3,600
E. Course development and piloting time (125 days @ $125)	15,625
F. Course materials development costs	2,000
G. DP training staff course presentation and miscellaneous administrative time (15 days @ 125)	1,875
H. Student course attendance time (25 students × 5 days @ $125)	15,625
I. Course materials and other course conduct expenses (25 students @ $25)	625
J. Use of facilities	125
K. Use of user time to assist in working up case study (5 days @ $125)	625
Total costs	$ 44,925

II. BENEFITS

A. Reduced turnover of systems analysts (3 @ $5000)	$ 15,000
B. Reduced turnover of DP training staff (1 @ $5000)	5,000
C. Increased professionalism of DP training staff	500
D. Residual value of systems analysis training course materials	2,000
E. Delivery of potential cost savings over status quo (10 percent of $8 million first-year savings)	800,000
F. Increased professionalism of systems analysis	5,000
G. Value of use of case study developed from OBB material	2,000
Total benefits	$829,500
Net benefits	$784,575

Alternative 3B: Vendor In-house Training

This alternative assumes that a DP training vendor will present a packaged, off-the-shelf, five-day systems analysis workshop at the OBB home offices.

CALCULATION OF VENDOR IN-HOUSE
TRAINING COSTS AND BENEFITS
I. COSTS

A. DP training staff time conducting research (5 days
@ $125) — $ 625

B. Public course review (5 days) (fee, travel and subsistence, and time) — 1,825

C. DP training staff time spent on vendor evaluation,
selection, negotiation, and student registration coordination (5 days @ $125) — 625

D. DP training staff time attending vendor in-house
course (5 days @ $125) — 625

E. Student course attendance time (25 students × 5
days @ $125) — 15,625

F. Course conduct expenses — 125

G. Use of facilities — 125

H. Vendor basic fee and expenses — 6,600

Total costs — $26,175

II. BENEFITS

A. Reduced turnover of systems analysts (3 @ $5000) — $ 15,000

B. Delivery of potential cost savings over status quo
(10 percent of $8 million first-year savings) — 800,000

C. Increased professionalism of systems analysts — 5,000

D. Increased availability of DP training staff — 500

Total benefits — $820,500

Net benefits — $794,325

Alternative 3C: Vendor Public Training

This alternative assumes that a DP training vendor presents systems
analysis workshops publicly to enable you to enroll 25 systems analysts
all at once or in smaller groups.

CALCULATION OF VENDOR PUBLIC
TRAINING COSTS AND BENEFITS
I. COSTS

A. DP training staff time conducting research (5 days
@ $125) — $ 625

Exhibit 2.2 (continued) _____

B.	Public course review (5 days) (fee, travel and subsistence, and time)	1,825
C.	DP training staff time spent on vendor evaluation, selection, and student registration coordination (5 days @ $125)	625
D.	Student course attendance time (25 students × 5 days @ $125)	15,625
E.	Vendor public course fee, student travel and subsistence (25 @ $1200)	30,000
F.	Cost associated with having systems analysts out of town during emergencies	1,000
	Total costs	$49,700

II. BENEFITS

A.	Reduced turnover of systems analysts (3 @ $5000)	$ 15,000
B.	Delivery of potential cost savings over status quo (10 percent of $8 million first-year savings)	800,000
C.	Increased professionalism of systems analysts	
D.	Availability of part of systems analyst group due to flexible scheduling	1,000
E.	Increased availability of DP training staff	500
	Total benefits	$816,500
	Net benefits	$766,800

SOME FINAL THOUGHTS ON COST-EFFECTIVENESS ANALYSIS. Many DP training directors have used cost-effectiveness analysis and failed. Why? Usually because they did not obtain DP or top management prior agreement on their assignment of values to noneconomic costs and benefits. Without prior agreement on these noneconomic or intangible factors, the cost-effectiveness analysis may be perceived as simply an elaborate mechanism to "prove in" just about anything the DP training director wants. Skeptics say, "Figures don't lie, but liars figure ... especially when they are doing DP training cost-effectiveness analyses." Avoid this problem by checking

Summary of Cost-effectiveness Analysis Findings

Here are the costs, benefits, and the net benefits (costs) associated with the five alternatives:

ALTERNATIVE	COST($)	BENEFIT($)	NET BENEFITS (COSTS)($)
1. Status quo	895,250	26,175	(869,075)
2. Consultants	832,500	1,051,175	218,675
3. A: Self-developed and presented training	44,925	829,500	784,575
B: Vendor in-house training	26,175	820,500	794,325
C: Vendor public training	49,700	816,500	766,800

RECOMMENDATION

Alternative 3B, vendor in-house training, is the most cost-effective alternative analyzed. According to the comparison of alternatives, it will have net benefits of $794,325.

your assumptions with those who have to "buy" your analysis—before presenting your results. You can see the importance of correct assumptions in the Exhibit 2.2 example. If top management had not agreed that the training could deliver $800,000 of potential cost savings over the status quo, then the results of the example analysis might have been significantly different.

Return on investment (ROI)

WHY USE ROI? Another form of hard cost justification is return on investment (ROI). This approach provides management with a realistic basis for making decisions relating to the alternative use of organizational resources including money, people's time, and computer facilities.

There are two forms of ROI that can be used by the DP training director: (1) ROI calculated from the results of a cost-effectiveness analysis; and (2) ROI using assumed productivity levels. The first approach is preferred over the second, but time constraints or other factors in many cases necessitate use of the second approach. Both of these methods assume productivity measurement at the "cost" level, rather than at the "revenue" level. Many organizations prefer to look at people productivity returns on the basis of how much revenue each person produces.

ROI USING COST-EFFECTIVENESS ANALYSIS. The return on the DP training investment is defined as the amount of benefit or cost savings that results from the investment of the training cost.

In the case of the training alternatives presented in Exhibit 2.2, assume that we have selected the most cost-effective alternative, vendor in-house training (alternative 3B in the example). What is the anticipated return on investment (ROI) from the planned investment in training? (See Exhibit 2.3 for details on the vendor in-house training alternative.)

Again, you can see the importance of correct assumptions in Exhibit 2.2. If top management had not agreed that the training could deliver $800,000 of potential cost savings over the status quo, then the results of this ROI calculation would be significantly different. In actual practice, the cost savings over status quo of each alternative under consideration in cost-effectiveness analysis could differ. This variation in cost savings per alternative would also produce significantly different ROI results.

*Exhibit 2.3: Rate of Return on Investment (ROI)*_____
Cost-Effectiveness Analysis

Here are the numbers:

1. The return on investment (ROI) from the use of vendor in-house systems analysis training from Exhibit 2.2 is $820,500. (Benefits to be generated by conducting the training.)

2. The cost of this training (TC) from Exhibit 2.2 is $26,175.

Here is the equation:

$$\text{Rate of return} = \frac{\text{ROI}}{\text{TC}}$$

$$\text{Rate of return} = \frac{\$820,500}{26,175}$$

Rate of return = 31.4 times *or* 3,140 percent

ROI USING ASSUMED PRODUCTIVITY LEVELS. If you have not completed a cost-effectiveness analysis, but you still want to cost justify DP training using the ROI approach, you may use the assumed level of productivity version of this approach. Using this version, you identify the return on the DP training investment as the difference in the productivity level of the DP staff *with training* and the productivity level of the DP staff *without training*. You must assume a productivity level for both these situations. You should obtain DP management's agreement with your assumptions.

If we use the same group of 25 systems analysts as discussed in Exhibit 2.2, we know that they have an average annual salary of $25,000 and an overhead assignment of 10 percent or $2,500. The fully loaded annual cost for the systems analyst team is $687,500 (25 systems analysts × $27,500). Everyone accepts the fact that in DP people's technical obsolescence is a serious problem. If, after one year, these 25 systems analysts will be operating at 95 percent of their current effectiveness, then we are probably blessed with an extraordinary group. At the end of the year after they are given the systems analysis training, they might be operating at 110 percent of their current effectiveness or productivity level.

Using these assumed productivity rates, let's calculate the ROI of the systems analysis training. Productivity value at the end of the year after training is $756,500 (110 percent of $687,500). Productivity value at the end of the year with no training is $618,750 (90 percent of $687,500). The difference in

---

Exhibit 2.4: Rate of Return on Investment (ROI) _____
Assumed Productivity Levels

Here are the numbers:
1. Systems analysis staff average annual salary is $25,000.
2. Overhead assignment on this salary is 10% or $2,500.
3. A fully loaded average annual salary is $27,500.
4. The total systems analysis team is made up of 25 people.
5. The total annual systems analysis team salary is $687,500 (25 × $27,500).
6. Staff productivity at the end of the year *with training* (PT) has a value of $756,500 (110% of $687,500).
7. Staff productivity at the end of the year *without training* (PW) has a value of $618,750 (90% of $687,500).
8. The *direct cost* of training (TD) is $6,600.

Here is the equation:

$$\text{Rate of return} = \frac{PT - PW}{TD}$$

$$\text{Rate of return} = \frac{\$756,500 - \$618,750}{6,600}$$

Rate of return = 20.8 times *or* 2,080 percent

these two productivity values is $137,500. This is the ROI for the systems analysis training. Using the *direct costs* for the in-house training course ($6,600), you may obtain an assumed rate of return of 20.8 times or 2,080 percent. This rate of return is not as high as the rate of return obtained from using the cost-effectiveness analysis figures, but it is close enough for most purposes. (See Exhibit 2.4.)

SOME FINAL THOUGHTS ON ROI. The financial leverage of DP training available to DP management is extremely high. As a skilled DP training director who has management's interests and objectives in mind, you will want to make management aware of this financial leverage. ROI is a tool that when used at the proper time can help you to accomplish this task.

Soft Cost-justification Approaches

Soft cost-justification approaches technically are not cost-justification approaches at all, but merely different ways of looking at the investment in DP training. They should be used to augment the hard approaches whenever possible. These soft approaches provide useful tools to give DP and top management a different perspective of money spent for DP training. This perspective should be useful at training budget time.

Keeping-up-with-the-Joneses

After a few years of experience, most DP managers know how to budget the systems and programming function. Usually the systems and programming budget is a function of the antici-pated new systems development and maintenance activity. This activity is determined by surveying users' needs for new computer-based applications and surveying present systems for updates and modifications. All in all, budgeting for a systems and programming organization is fairly complex, but it has been done so many times that it is relatively easy for DP management to do. Budgeting for DP training is quite another thing.

Many fledgling DP training directors have agonized over the detailed cost breakdowns of every line item in their training budgets only to have the bottom line slashed by a fixed percentage ... just because it looked out of line. Many DP managers have asked, "How does our DP training budget compare to others in the industry? Or to other organizations of our size?" When they ask these questions, DP managers are using the keeping-up-with-the-Joneses approach to DP training budgeting.

The keeping-up-with-the-Joneses budgeting method is far from the best, but if it is the only way to obtain your DP training budget, then you'd better use it. How do you know what the Joneses are spending? There is an available source of information on the subject—Appendix A, the *1977–1978 BSI Annual DP Training Survey*. You should obtain a copy of this survey each year and keep it in your DP training budget file. This way you will know how your DP training budget compares to other organizations like yours in case your DP manager asks.

Table 2.1 presents an expansion of the results of the latest survey questions relating to DP staff size, DP budget, and DP training budget. This information was taken from the spread sheets of data compiled, summarized, and interpreted in the latest *BSI Annual DP Training Survey*. The table will show you how your DP training budget compares to organizations having about the same DP staff size and DP budget as your organization.

Structured versus unstructured training

The DP industry can use another "structured" idea so why not *structured training*? In fairness to the training profession, however, structured training was here long before structured programming. Structured training simply means formal train-

Table 2.1: Keeping-up-with-the Joneses
(1977–78 BSI Annual DP Training Survey, expansion of questions 6, 7, 8)

No Firms	DP Staff Size	DP Budget ($) Range		DP Budget ($) Reported		DP Training Budget ($) Range		DP Training Budget ($) Reported	
		Low	High	Avg.	Adjusted Mean*	Low	High	Avg.	Adjusted Mean*
4	25 or less	417K	600K	554K	600K	0	8K	6K	6K
4	26–50	1M	1.7M	1.4M	1.25M	5K	20K	10.25K	8K
9	51–75	972K	8M	2.4M	2.6M	12K	100K	39.8K	38K
8	76–100	1.4M	5M	3.9M	4.1M	35K	215K	84.7K	68.5K
21	101–150	388K	7.5M	4.5M	4.6M	20K	140K	79.3K	78.8K
14	151–200	3M	9.8M	6.1M	6.0M	13K	800K	143.2K	90.5K
6	201–250	6.8M	16M	9.7M	8.0M	60K	150K	118.3K	112.4K
7	251–300	5M	15M	10.0M	10.0M	14K	235K	102.7K	94.0K
5	301–400	1.5M	8.5M	5.0M	5.0M	62K	250K	165.5K	175.0K
16	over 400	10M	47.5M	25.3M	24.6M	1K	380K	207.5K	210.0K
94 Total									

K = thousands
M = millions
*Adjusted mean is the arithmetic mean of the reported budgets after the lowest and the highest budgets within the category have been eliminated.

ing. Unstructured training often means on-the-job (OJT) training. (Although properly conducted OJT may not be "instructional" at all.)

If you do not have a structured DP training program, you will find it very hard to cost justify the training. Having a structured training program assumes that you have taken the time to conduct a task analysis, establish training course objectives, and develop or acquire training programs to meet those objectives. On the other hand, unstructured training is often hit-or-miss impulse training.

Many DP organizations rely heavily on unstructured training. There is nothing wrong with unstructured training, except it is not predictable, and it may be a very expensive way of training DP professionals to accomplish certain tasks. DP management might not view unstructured training as training at all. And they might not view the costs associated with it as training costs. This is why using the comparative approach to justifying DP training can prove useful in some cases.

How do you use structured versus unstructured to justify DP training? First, show DP management that the cost to conduct unstructured training has a real and identifiable dollar value. Also show that, for all practical purposes, this number is fixed for each student trained using unstructured training. Suppose, for example, you wanted to identify the cost of using unstructured training to teach the systems department people to use the techniques of structured design and programming. You would study the amount of time spent by supervisors and project managers in sharing their knowledge of structured design and programming skills with their subordinates. You would measure the time each subordinate spends experimenting with the new techniques and the abortive computer test time expended in attempts to use the new technique. Finally, you might measure the number of bugs found in newly structured programs.

Let's assume that you were able to show that it costs $500

per student to teach structured design and programming using the unstructured training approach. What would it cost to train people to use structured design and programming using a structured training method? Assume that a structured design and programming workshop meeting your requirements could be acquired for $6,600, and that this fee covers up to 25 students. Having this information will enable you to show DP management graphically how to view the two forms of training.

Exhibit 2.5 uses the figures presented above to illustrate a cost comparison of these training methods. To some DP

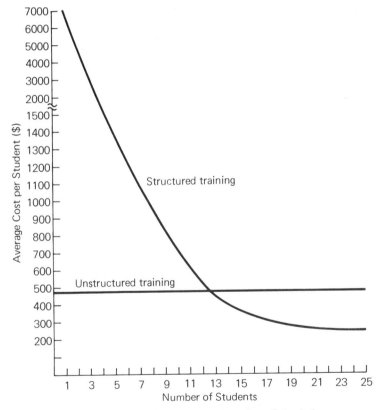

Figure 2.5: Structured versus unstructured training

training directors, this is a clear and convincing method of cost justifying the use of structured versus unstructured training. It certainly is another tool to assist you in justifying your DP training budget.

Awareness-experimentation-adoption model

DP managers often ask, "Can't we cover all that those students need to know in a three-day workshop rather then have them off the job for the five-day workshop?" Naturally, the correct answer to the question is yes. But, you should add... "at a price." The awareness-experimentation-adoption model of learning, originally established by Don Ricks,* should help you educate DP managers to be sensitive to the cost of "exposing" people to a subject rather than "teaching" them the subject. Remember, George Odiorne says that giving someone "exposure" to a subject is nothing more than "pedagogical streaking."

Naturally, how long a student should be trained on a subject has a lot to do with the primary training objective. If you are simply trying to give the student an awareness of the subject area, a pedagogical streaking might be all the student requires. If you want the student to adopt new skills, knowledge, or attitudes taught by the course, then the student must have time to experiment with them in a simulated or real job situation. This experiment can be facilitated by the use of workshop exercises, case study examples, and teamwork course organization. This is the essence of the awareness-experimentation-adoption learning model.

How can this model be used to help you justify a DP training budget which is often made up of costs for five-day

---

*Don M. Ricks, a former English professor turned trainer, is president of IWCC Ltd. in Calgary, Alberta, a firm that specializes in helping people improve their letter and report writing skills. Ricks discusses the awareness-experimentation-learning model further in the June 1978 issue of *Training HRD* magazine.

workshops? Exhibit 2.6 demonstrates the economics of awareness versus adoption. This is another tool which gives a different perspective of DP training cost and effectiveness. According to Ricks, the adoption of skills, knowledge, and attitudes depends on the duration of a training course. This relationship is illustrated by the curve in Exhibit 2.6. If training costs $1,000 per day for up to 20 students, what is the apparent cost per student for a one-day, two-day, three-day, four-day, or five-day course? Assuming a typical percentage of students adopt the skills, knowledge, or attitudes taught by the training, what is the actual cost per student for courses of those durations?

Table 2.2 illustrates the course economics represented by the curve in Exhibit 2.6. This illustration might prove that the most cost-effective course duration is somewhere between four and five days. This can be viewed as the point of maximum return, because the actual cost per student truly trained is at its lowest level here.

Training efficiency equation

The training efficiency equation, originally discussed by

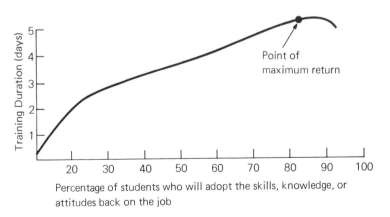

Figure 2.6: Awareness-experimentation-adoption model

Table 2.2

Course Duration	Number of Students	Course Cost	Apparent Cost per Student	Number and Percentage of Students who Adopted Skills, Knowledge, or Attitudes	Actual Cost per Student Truly Trained
One day	20	$1000	$ 50	2 (10%)	$500
Two days	20	2000	100	5 (20%)	400
Three days	20	3000	150	10 (50%)	300
Four days	20	4000	200	15 (75%)	265
Five days	20	5000	250	17 (85%)	295

Cullen and Sanzin,* is as much a tool for educating DP training directors as it is a tool for educating DP managers. Often the basic logic of this equation is overlooked by DP training directors.

The logic of the training efficiency equation is overlooked when organizations, in the name of efficiency, spend less on training while keeping their students in the training course longer. These organizations seem to be hoping that added learning will miraculously take place if the students are "overexposed" to a shallow presentation of a course subject. This happens frequently in DP organizations where the training director's performance is measured by the amount of DP training activity, rather than by the amount of DP training effectiveness.

In these DP organizations, it is often thought that cutting training costs (development and/or presentation) by half and doubling student hours makes training more efficient or effective. Such actions usually have the opposite effect. The training efficiency equation should always be in the back of

---

*For complete reference to the Cullen and Sanzin discussion of this subject, refer to the bibliography.

your mind when checking your training costs against the number of student days.

Once DP management accepts the training efficiency equation perspective of viewing training duration versus effectiveness, the components of this equation can be used specifically to justify a high-quality (thus more cost-effective) training alternative. See Exhibit 2.7 for an illustration of this cost justification approach.

This is another tool to help you to educate DP management about economic realities of DP training.

Summary

Before you are ready to move ahead with cost justifying DP training, you should invest some time in DP management education. Knowing what is required from all participants in the justification process is essential for cost justification to succeed.

Cost-justification approaches are either hard or soft approaches. Hard justification approaches should be used whenever attempting to justify an important DP training program, *and* you have the necessary time and data. Soft justification approaches may be used to provide DP management with different perspectives relating to the economics of DP training. Soft-justification approaches should be used in conjunction with hard-justification approaches to ensure maximum success from DP cost-justification efforts.

Cost-effectiveness analysis and return on investment (ROI) are two hard cost-justification approaches. Soft cost-justification approaches include: (1) keeping-up-with-the-Joneses; (2) structured versus unstructured training; (3) awareness-experimentation-adoption model; and (4) training efficiency equation.

Once you have mastered DP training cost justification you are ready to tackle the difficult problem of DP training effectiveness measurement and evaluation.

Exhibit 2.7: Training Efficiency Equation _____

The equation is:

$$\text{Training efficiency} = \frac{\begin{array}{c}\text{Student Cost}\\ \text{(student hours in training)}\end{array}}{\begin{array}{c}\text{Training Cost}\\ \text{(development and/or presentation)}\end{array}}$$

Here is an example of how the components of the training efficiency equation can be used to justify the right DP training course. This is the problem:

1. There are 25 students who will each spend 5 days in a systems analysis workshop.

2. The fully loaded daily cost for their time is $125.

3. The direct cost for this training presented by Vendor A is $6,600. Vendor A's course is a high-quality, proven workshop course.

4. The direct cost for this training presented by Vendor B is $3,300. Vendor B's course is a low-quality, shallow overview of systems analysis.

5. DP management insists on Vendor B who will bring the training to the DP department at "half the cost."

This is the question: Is DP management right?

The answer: No.

Here is why:

1. The total training costs using Vendor A will be:

Student costs (25 students × 5 days @ $125)	$15,625
Training costs	6,600
Total Vendor A Course Costs	$22,225

2. The total training costs using Vendor B will be:

Student costs (25 students × 5 days @ $125)	$15,625
Training costs	3,300
Total Vendor B Course Costs	$18,925

3. The cost savings achieved by selecting Vendor B over Vendor A is 14.9%, <u>not</u> 50%:

$$\text{Savings (as a percentage of overall course cost)} = \frac{\text{Cost Savings}}{\text{Total Vendor A Course Cost}}$$

$$\text{Savings} = \frac{\$\ 3,300}{\$22,225} = 14.9\%$$

(As an added observation, training efficiency might better compare a five-day course with a three-day course of apparent comparable quality. This is often the choice given to organizations seeking a training course solution to a problem. It may not be realistic to assume that any organization would deliberately choose to present a "poor" training course, despite its low cost.)

CHAPTER 3

HOW TO MEASURE
AND EVALUATE
DP TRAINING
EFFECTIVENESS

Preliminary Thoughts

While DP training cost justification is important, ensuring that the selected DP training program delivers the promised return on the investment is critical. Properly cost justified training that fails to meet its anticipated objectives can be extremely damaging to overall DP organizational effectiveness and to the credibility of DP training.

A pragmatic system of measurement and evaluation of DP training effectiveness must be a part of the preliminary thinking and design of every DP training program. The products of this measurement and evaluation effort should be constantly fed back to DP management to show whether or not their decision to invest in DP training continues to bring them the financial returns that were anticipated. If this return on investment falls off, DP management should be told as quickly as possible to enable them to make proper decisions concerning how DP personnel should be employed.

Management Education Requirements

By far, more information has been written on the subject of measuring and evaluating training than on the subject of cost justifying training. Many of these well-documented measurement and evaluation approaches are directly applicable to DP training. When preparing to measure and evaluate the results of your DP training program, you should study the methods employed by others who have measured similar programs.

However, it is possible to copy other people's approaches, but not their results. This is an important concept to communicate to DP management. Your measurement and evaluation efforts must be specific to your organization because it is made up of unique personalities, unique business requirements, and unique problems.

Recently, a group of blue-ribbon training directors met in Chicago for the purpose of discussing how they could better prove productivity results from the investment in DP training. Specifically, the group met to achieve three objectives:

Determine if it is possible to demonstrate the impact of an internal DP training program on staff productivity.

Review experiences of the attendees in attempting to document this relationship.

Establish a plan of action for a project to produce the documentation desired.

The organizers of the meeting hoped that bringing together a number of seasoned DP training directors for this meeting would lead to the identification of methods to prove that DP training could indeed be shown to increase productivity in terms of increased correct lines of code, fewer operator errors, reduced program bugs, and so on.

Unfortunately, the meeting did not accomplish these desired objectives. After a long period of sharing and discussion, the consensus was that "DP trainers should continue to measure the effectiveness of DP training courses, but should not try to relate this training effectiveness to productivity gains." This was a discouraging outcome to many in attendance. (Perhaps a relief to others!) As DP training professionals, we should not stop *trying* to show that training relates to productivity improvement; however, we should be realistic about what we can *prove* to DP management.

We should make every effort to educate DP management to appreciate the limitation of training measurement and evaluation. DP management should be educated to understand that, while, ideally, DP training *should* improve DP department productivity, it will probably be extremely difficult for the DP training director to prove it. If management insists on proof, the best you can do is offer them the strongest circumstantial evidence possible that your program is delivering as promised. One good way to document this evidence is to have an effective measurement and evaluation mechanism designed into every DP training program *before* sending the first student through the course. Having such a mechanism established before the training demands the cooperation, involvement, and support of management right from the start. "Proving" the effectiveness of training may boil down to agreement on financial assumptions that involve DP management to a considerable degree.

The fear that DP management will expect too much from training measurement and evaluation is offset in some DP organizations by the reality that management expects too little from DP training in general and from training measurement and evaluation in particular. DP managers in these organizations tend to leave training alone. These DP managers may view training with a lack of commitment that results in DP training being funded by "anyway accounting." Each year the DP manager issues a statement to the effect that "the three people in the DP training group are on the payroll, so what does it matter what they do. We are going to pay them anyway." This is called "anyway accounting."

In these organizations, if DP managers ask questions at all about training, they usually ask the wrong questions. Unfortunately, many DP training directors dutifully provide the answers to these wrong questions by submitting their annual training activities reports. These wrong questions are questions like, How many courses were conducted last year? To how many students? What was the cost per student? These kinds of questions may be fine for computer operations where activity is an important measure of efficiency; they are quantitative questions, not qualitative questions. The challenge to training directors in these organizations is to educate DP management to ask the "right," qualitative, performance analysis questions like, Who, why, what, how, and what was the change in behavior? Having a DP manager who expects too little or one who expects too much from DP training are touchy problems that must be tackled by a good education program for DP management. Only when you strike a proper balance between these extremes can you be assured of a successful measurement and evaluation program and, hence, a successful DP training program.

Laying the Groundwork

To establish a successful DP training measurement and evaluation program involves everyone in the DP department. Before the job of measurement and evaluation can be done satisfactorily, everyone who will participate in or manage the training program has to be convinced of its value.

The involvement and participation of all supervisors in the DP department is especially important. This involvement is so essential to one Florida DP organization that it has appointed a "school board" to oversee the training program. This board is made up of top DP management and the DP training director. The board attempts to evaluate all DP training and to associate its evaluations with the organization's active performance improvement program. This organization believes that commitment to DP training measurement and evaluation are essential.

Peter Drucker once said, "The key to making the human resource more productive is not training. That comes second. The first requirement is to make sure that people can do the work they are being paid for, then you train them." There are a number of reasons why people in a DP organization may not be doing the work they are being paid for. Poor supervision, poor job placement, poor working conditions, inadequate salary and fringe benefits, or the wrong management style or philosophy are all reasons for poor people performance. No amount of training can improve the productivity of certain people who are working under certain circumstances. The DP training director must be sure that training is the correct solution to the problem that needs solving.

If training is the solution to the problem, then it's time to make sure you have identified the right training solution. As mentioned, this requires developing and maintaining a comprehensive task analysis of the DP department, accompanied by a comprehensive skills analysis to identify the knowledge or attitude needs of your organization. Set the DP training course objectives and, only then, select the training course.

Before conducting the training, you should ensure that you have agreed with DP management on the standards of accomplishment that will measure the effectiveness of every training course. Setting these measurement standards will often require you to go back to each task identified in your task analysis to establish a task standard against which job performance can be measured. For example, if one of your tasks is, "Code computer programs using COBOL," then the accompanying task standard might be, "...at an average rate of 25 statements an hour."

The final task and skills analysis effort should result in three products:

Identification of DP training course objectives

Identification of required skills, knowledge, and attitudes

Standards for valid performance measurement

If this is accomplished with the agreement of DP department management and potential students, then your attempts to measure and evaluate DP training stand a much better chance of being successful.

Proper accomplishment of DP task analysis, including the identification of task standards, links training with department performance improvement in such a way that DP training will stop being viewed as the department "schoolhouse," and start being viewed as the department "performance improver." However, do not forget the limitations of DP training evaluation and measurement by betting that you can prove that successful DP training leads to improved performance. Why?

First of all, training is often not an appropriate solution to a performance problem. For example, a project team's morale and productivity will take a quantum leap upward when a difficult user manager is transferred. Or, a simple decision to establish a career development program, including task analysis and career paths, can lead to an immediate jump in overall department performance improvement.

Recent studies show that factors as simple as the amount of smiling and complimenting done by first-line supervisors can improve subordinate productivity by as much as 60 percent. Don't forget the Hawthorne effect. E. C. Keachie put it this way: "Difficulties in the evaluation of training are evident at the outset in the problem technically called 'the separation of variables,' that is, how much improvement is due to training as compared to other factors."

One of the most important pieces of groundwork that you

must lay is to obtain DP management's approval to spend your time and money on DP training measurement and evaluation. If the measurement and evaluation job is to be done correctly, it requires a considerable investment of DP training and DP department resources. Do not underestimate the cost of proper evaluation. Ensure initially that this expenditure is reflected in your cost justification of the DP training course to be certain that those people who will make the decision to move ahead with the training are familiar with the necessity and cost of proper DP training measurement and evaluation.

At this time, you should also obtain agreement on the roles of the participants involved in this measurement and evaluation effort. Who are they? When do you need their assistance? How much of their time do you need? Will you have to negotiate any issues? Who should resolve any disagreements? Get these details pinned down early to avoid having the pressures of the training need interfere with proper preparation for measurement and evaluation.

Another important piece of groundwork is to establish the measurement and evaluation objectives. Why are you doing it in the first place? Do you plan to repeat this training? Should improvements be made to the training course based on the results? Will your measurement and evaluation efforts mean that students might receive additional training? Obtain complete agreement on why you are doing measurement and evaluation before committing time and money.

Exhibit 3.1 graphically illustrates the steps that should be taken before you are ready to measure and evaluate DP training.

What and How to Measure

Now that we have established the appropriate groundwork for DP training measurement and evaluation, what is it that we want to measure and evaluate?

Don Kirkpatrick is one of the most practical advocates of technical training measurement and evaluation in the country today. His approach is easily adapted to DP training. The remaining pages of this chapter translate the Kirkpatrick model into a set of practical tools for DP training directors to conduct measurement and evaluation and to educate DP management in this process.

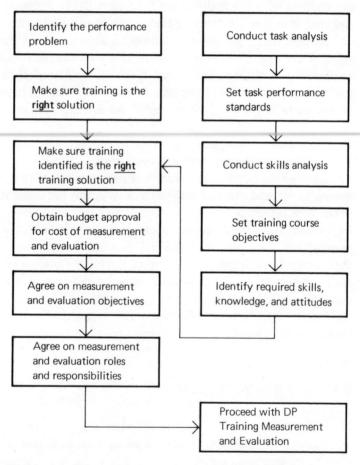

Figure 3.1: Steps before measurement and evaluation

DP training measurement and evaluation should measure the effectiveness of DP training in terms of four dimensions:

Reaction

Learning

Behavior

Results

The following paragraphs define these dimensions and tell how to measure them in DP training.

Reaction

Measurement of students' reaction to a DP training course is done simply to find out how they feel about such a course immediately after its completion. The measurement mechanism to accomplish this is usually the student reaction, course evaluation, or comment sheets. This form is in common use in most DP training organizations. In addition to asking students what they thought about a DP training course, the form is often used to obtain their reaction to course facilities, student meals, instructor teaching abilities, instructor knowledge of the subject, and so on. For some reason, DP training directors seem to have an affinity for student reaction sheets which associate happy faces with good marks and frowning faces with bad marks. The form of the reaction sheet is not as important as the use the form is put to. Measuring student reaction to a training course is relatively easy. The simple evaluation form can prove how the students reacted to the course, provided they are giving their honest opinions.

When a training course on an organization's DP standards is presented by the DP manager and students are asked to submit their "honest" reactions to the session *and* sign their names, can this result in an honest response? Without honesty built into the mechanism to measure reaction, the results cannot be evaluated as proof of the measurement of the reaction dimension of DP training.

Here is another important rule. If you do not plan to consider students' suggestions for improvements, often solicited by reaction forms, do not ask for them. There is no worse way to ruin your credibility with your constituents than to leave a problem in a DP training course uncorrected after several students have been asked for their suggestions, given them, and then been ignored.

Measuring student reaction to a training course is important, and you should do this if nothing else. Keep in mind, however, that students can have a good reaction to a training course and still not learn anything.

Learning

In measuring the learning dimension of DP training, you must keep in mind that students will learn new skills, knowledge, or attitudes in a DP training course. Most DP training courses provide a mixture of these three kinds of learning, with one of the three prevailing in the course design. For example, a "Structured Design and Programming Workshop" will predominately teach systems designers new *skills* in the structured approach to systems design and programming. An "Introduction to DP" taught to keypunch operators will predominately provide the *knowledge* of where keypunchers fit into the big picture of DP. A "User's Guide to Systems Development" course will predominately be used to change or influence the *attitudes* of users toward their roles and responsibilities in the systems development process. The dominant type of learning delivered by the DP training course will determine how that course should be measured and evaluated, and whether the results of the measurement can be considered proof (or merely evidence) that the desired learning has taken place.

One of the easiest ways to measure learning is to ask students if they learned anything from the training course.

Students may give their answers orally or in writing. Often students are positively impressed when the DP training director interviews them personally upon completion of the course. If you have time, personal interviewing is the preferred approach.

Testing is another way to measure learning. Testing for skills and knowledge acquired is always easier than testing for new attitudes learned. Testing should involve pretesting and posttesting to ascertain the difference in skills, knowledge, or attitudes before and after the course. Tests are often designed into a training course as a feedback mechanism for DP management. DP organizations must be cautious in their use of tests. Tests used for recruitment, promotion, or salary reviews should be fully validated for job relevance to meet government rules regarding equal employment opportunity.

Another method of measuring student learning is classroom observation. This is particularly effective in workshop courses where students demonstrate their newly acquired skill or knowledge as a part of the learning process.

Measuring learning by student interviewing, testing, and classroom observation as discussed above will give you evidence of learning, but not proof. This evidence is somewhat difficult to come by, but by no means impossible. Gathering evidence of learning should be a routine measurement and evaluation activity of every DP training organization.

If you need to obtain proof of learning, you must eliminate all the variables *except* the training from the measured results and evaluation. This may only be accomplished by pretesting and posttesting both an experimental group (a group of students who attended the training course) and a control group (a similar group of DP people who did not attend the training course). If the results of your testing show the experimental group has in fact learned more than the control group, then this is proof that the experimental group has learned from the course. Obtaining proof in this way is quite difficult and costly, but not impossible. When DP managers insist on proof of learning, this approach is the only reliable method of providing the proof that they desire.

Behavior

Obtaining evidence of behavior change on the job as a dimension of DP training measurement is not particularly difficult. All you have to do is to ask the students whether or not their behavior changed as a result of the training course once they got back on the job. Better yet, ask a student's supervisor whether that student's behavior changed back on the job. This measurement can be accomplished by pretests and posttests, questionnaires, and interviews. After DP training, students who have reacted well to the course and who have apparently learned a lot as a result of it sometimes do not change their behavior when they arrive back on the job. This is a common source of "black eyes" for DP training. These cases may often be explained by factors that have nothing to do with the training, or that student's reaction, or learning as a result of the course.

Ask the student's supervisor a few questions. Will it be to the student's advantage to improve by using the new techniques learned in the course? What does the supervisor think of the course subject? Is the environment sympathetic to the use of the new skill? (This is a frequent problem with structured programming.) Will the student be able to experiment with the new skill without inordinate risk? Will the student get help or support when needed? If the answers to these questions are negative, you can establish the real reason why the student's behavior on the job did not change.

If your DP manager insists on your proving that the training course changed student behavior back on the job, you may be in for a long, complicated, and costly measurement process. This is the kind of process that is seldom undertaken except by very large DP organizations with sizeable training staffs. To provide that behavior has changed back on the job because of the training course, you must accomplish three things:

Measure student behavior before the training course.

Measure student behavior after the training course.

Prove that the change in behavior resulted from the DP training course and not some other factor.

Measurement of behavior can be accomplished by testing, interviews, questionnaries, and observation. This process is extremely costly, so be sure to place a considerable sum in your DP training budget if you are required to prove behavior change. Even if you carry out the measurement of behavior change, it is not clear that present-day techniques will ensure adequate results to claim that you have proof.

Results

Most DP managers who are not educated about the realistic limitations of DP training measurement and evaluation want proof that training provides results in terms of increased

Table 3.1: Difficulty in Applying Training Effectiveness Measurement and Evaluation to DP Training _____

When Measuring for...	To obtain...	
	Evidence	*Proof*
1. Reaction	Easy	So-So
2. Learning	So-So	Hard
3. Behavior change	Hard and costly	Impractical, if not impossible, very costly
4. Results	Extremely hard and very costly	Impossible

Table 3.2: Tools Available for Measuring the Effectiveness of DP Training

	To Obtain...	
	Evidence	*Proof*
Reaction	1. Reaction forms 2. Student evaluation forms 3. Course review forms	1. *Honest* reaction forms
Learning	1. Pretest and posttest 2. Classroom observation 3. Student questionnaires 4. Student and supervisor interviews	1. Pretest and posttest of experimental control 2. Classroom observation 3. Student questionnaires 4. Student and supervisor interviews
Behavior Change	1. Pretest and posttest using experimental and control groups 2. Student and supervisor interviews 3. Behavioral change tests	1. Tests and interviews to: a. Measure behavior before b. Measure behavior after 2. Proof that no other variables interceded
Results	Same as "behavior change," but more complex because of variables	Same as "behavior change" but more complex because of variables

department productivity. Measuring this dimension of DP training is extremely difficult, so, unfortunately, you cannot prove those results for them. There are simply too many variables that come into play between training and ultimate performance results. Even to obtain evidence is very difficult and expensive. You must use a control group against an experimental group. The results of a rather complicated measurement activity will merely provide evidence, not proof, of

**Table 3.3: How Far to Go with DP Training,
Measurement, and Evaluation** _____

Courses Teaching Predominately...

Skills	Knowledge	Attitudes
Such as:	Such as:	Such as:
Structured Design Programming Workshop	Introduction to DP	Users Guide to Systems Development
JCL Workshop	Management of Structured Programming	Transactional Analysis
Design Techniques Workshop	An Overview of Distributed Processing	Planning for Computer Security

You Should Not Try to Go Further Than Obtaining...

Evidence of behavior change	Evidence of learning	Evidence of learning
or	*or*	*or*
Proof of learning	Proof of learning	Proof of reaction

results. The best interests of the DP department are served when you convince the manager to be content with evidence of learning and behavior change back on the job.

Applying Measurement and Evaluation to Training

To show how measurement and evaluation apply to DP training, three questions are presented below:

1. How difficult is it to apply these tools to DP training to obtain evidence and proof? Table 3.1 gives the answer to this question.

2. What tools are available to help a DP training director measure the four dimensions of training effectiveness? Table 3.2 summarizes the tools used to measure DP training for evidence and proof of effectiveness.

3. Realistically, how much measuring and evaluating should an average DP training director attempt? It depends on the kind of course you are measuring. Going back to the three categories of predominant learning that typify DP training courses, Table 3.3 shows how far to attempt to demonstrate evidence or proof of DP training effectiveness.

Summary

Although much is written on the subject of training measurement and evaluation, it is probably understood less by top managers, including DP managers, than any other aspect of training. Un-informed DP managers either expect too much from DP training or expect too little.

DP training directors must educate DP managers to ask the right questions and to have realistic expectations for DP training measurement and evaluation. DP training effectiveness should be measured by four dimensions: (1) reaction, (2) learning, (3) behavior change, and (4) results. Obtaining evidence of training effectiveness in these categories is not as difficult or as expensive as obtaining proof.

DP management must be aware of how to set up a measurement and evaluation program and what it will cost. Applying measurement to DP involves ascertaining whether the course mainly teaches skills, knowledge, or attitude change.

CHAPTER 4

SPOT-CHECKING
YOUR ORGANIZATION

How Do You Stand?

If you have read and adopted the first chapters of this book, you should know how to cost justify, measure, and evaluate DP training. Where does that leave you? In general, you are in pretty good shape. It puts you in the top 5 percent of DP training directors and in the top 20 percent of general training directors.

What's next? You have to be organized to establish and direct an effective DP training program. Before you get organized, you should find out how you stand within your DP department as compared to training directors in other DP departments, *and* you should continue to educate yourself in ways to do your job more professionally.

First, take the self-appraisal quiz presented in the next section. Second, read Appendix A, *1977–78 BSI Annual DP*

Training Survey and Appendix B, Tips for Trainers: Excerpts from the *BSI Insider News*. Third, join or help organize a DP training directors group in your DP community to share common problems and training resources with fellow directors. Appendix C, How to Organize a DP Training Directors Group in Your DP Community, offers some guidelines.

The Self-appraisal Quiz

Ask yourself the questions which follow below. If you know the answers and the answers are favorable, you are ready to launch an effective DP training program. If you fail the quiz, it may be time for you to have a talk with your DP manager about where DP training fits in the plans for your DP organization and in your personal career path.

What percentage of your DP budget is spent on DP training?

Answer: On the average, the DP training budgets of DP organizations make up 1.5 percent of the average DP budget. The breakdown of this figure by DP budget and staff size is shown in Table 2.1. If your training budget is less than 1.5 percent of your DP budget, then ask yourself why. Check to see if your organization differs for good reason or because there is no DP management commitment to DP training. (See Appendix A, *1977–78 BSI Annual DP Training Survey*.)

Do you have a full-time trainer for every 100 people?

Answer: On the average, DP organizations have one full-time, dedicated trainer for every 100 people. If you have over 100 people in your organization, and you are not able to devote full attention to DP training, then ask yourself why. Is your organization really committed to an effective DP training program? (See Appendix A, *1977–78 BSI Annual DP Training Survey.*)

When do you submit your DP training budget?

Answer: Most DP organizations prepare their training budgets in the last half of the calendar year. These budgets are usually funded as an overhead function of the DP department. If you must submit your budget at the same time as the DP department budget, you may not be budgeting properly. How can you know what the requirements will be for DP training until you know what is approved in the DP department's head count and budget? If there are major expenditures in the DP department's budget for new applications system development or for new hardware, then the requirements for DP training may be increased significantly.

Do you report DP training activity or performance?

Answer: Preparing a report to DP management covering your activities for the quarter or year is a must, providing the report answers DP management's "qualitative" as well as "quantitative" questions. If you are still reporting only your activity (number of students, courses, hours, and so on) and not attempting to report performance, you may be encouraging your DP manager to continue to ask the wrong questions of DP training.

Do you try to solve performance problems or just offer DP training?

Answer: If you look upon and recommend training as the solution to every performance problem in your DP organization, you may be doing the organization and yourself a disservice. Training is seldom the only solution to a performance problem. Make it your job to challenge every request for training to make sure that training is the right solution. Once you have done this successfully a few times, your constituents will see you as a person interested and knowledgeable in the area of performance improvement, not as just the principal of the "DP department schoolhouse."

Does DP training in your organization involve three phases: pretraining, training, and posttraining?

Answer: If your DP management and staff see training as a three-phased process, you are well prepared to do an effective DP training job. DP training should involve several steps before training, such as setting the proper training objectives, agreeing on the measurement and evaluation criteria, and pretesting and interviewing students. Supervisors should tell the students who work for them what they expect the students to learn from the DP training course. After the course, students, their supervisors, and the training director should communicate to ensure that the course did the expected job. Students and supervisors should be encouraged to participate in this sort of joint feedback session. This three-phased approach will greatly improve the effectiveness of the training *and* increase your credibility as DP training director.

Have members of your DP training staff, including yourself, been trained to do their jobs more effectively?

Answer: DP trainers tend to be the most undertrained of the professionals in the department. Each DP trainer should be trained in three areas for professional growth. They are: (1) DP human resource development; (2) administration of the DP training function; and (3) how to conduct a DP training course (a "train the trainer" course). These courses are available through DP training vendors including BSI and Deltak, and through the American Society of Training and Development (ASTD). Your job is too important to be conducted in a less than fully professional manner.

Do you cost justify DP training?

Answer: After reading this book, you know all the reasons for doing it and how to do it. If you still cannot do it for some reason, your DP training program is in serious danger of disappearing with the next economic downturn.

Do you measure and evaluate the effectiveness of DP training?

Answer: After reading this book, you also know all the reasons for doing measurement and evaluation and how to do it. If, for some reason, you still cannot do it, the long-term prognosis for your DP training program is grim.

What is your reporting responsibility?

Answer: There should not be more than one person between you and the top manager in the DP department. Ideally, as training director, you should report directly to the DP manager. This is one good way to ensure top-level commitment and involvement in training that characterizes the better programs. If the DP training function is relegated to a lower echelon of administration or is divided among several entities within the DP department, chances for a successful, effective, coordinated training program are greatly lessened. If you are not a fully dedicated DP trainer and your organization has more than 100 people, chances are, you cannot serve your organization effectively, regardless of your budget.

Do you know how much of your DP training budget is spent on each category of people (programmers, system analysts, etc.) within DP? How does it compare to what other DP organizations spend?

Answer: Each year the *BSI Annual DP Training Survey* asks this question and the answers are published and distributed at no cost to DP training directors. Check the survey results to see how you compare. If you spend far less or far more on one category of people, be sure you know the reason for it. If you do not know why, you should check your assumptions and confer with your DP manager about redistributing your training budget. (See Appendix A, *1977–78 BSI Annual DP Training Survey.*)

Have you implemented a human resource development (or career development) program in your DP department?

Answer: In the long run, the chances for success for a DP training program are greatly improved if it is an integral part of a DP human resource development (or career development) program. There are only a few DP organizations who have fully implemented such programs. These organizations benefit from reduced turnover, improved people productivity, better morale, and more organizational growth and maturity. A DP human resource development program should be made up of these elements:

1. Policy of advancement based on performance
2. Modern, active promotion appraisal program
3. Policy of promotion from within
4. Salary policy which is tied to performance appraisal
5. Organizational charter for DP training and development
6. Task and skills analyses
7. Task performance standards
8. DP training program including cost justification, measurement, and evaluation
9. Continuous recruitment program

Many DP organizations start with training first, then evolve into these other components of an overall human resource development program. If you are a relatively mature DP training organization, but you have not gone to the next level, you may want to consider the potential payoff of a fully integrated human resource development program for your DP organization.

Summary

If you have read the previous chapters of this book, you know the value of DP training cost justification and measurement and evaluation. However, you may not be ready to take advantage of these approaches unless you are organized for effective DP training. To find out whether you are ready for an effective DP training program, ask yourself the questions in the self-appraisal quiz. If you know the answers and the answers are favorable, you're ready. Keep abreast of the annual survey (Appendix A), read the tips to trainers (Appendix B), and help to organize a DP training directors group in your DP community (Appendix C).

With a concerted effort on the part of the DP training director and the DP manager, a truly professional training program can be a reality for your organization.

APPENDIX A

1977–78
BSI ANNUAL
DP TRAINING
SURVEY

Interpreted Results

Background

Each year, Brandon Systems Institute, Inc. (BSI) conducts its *Annual DP Training Survey*, summarizes, compiles, and interprets the results. These interpreted results are then made available to BSI clients and other interested people in the DP industry. BSI provides the *Survey* and its results as a free service to the DP industry of which it has been a part since 1964. Additional copies of this year's results may be obtained at no cost from:

Brandon Systems Institute, Inc.
4720 Montgomery Lane
Bethesda, Maryland 20014
(301)986-8611

This 1977–78 *Annual DP Training Survey* was conducted during November and December of 1977. The *Survey* results were then compiled, interpreted, and published in February of 1978. Completed questionnaires were received from 98 organizations, a sizeable increase over the 70 responses to the 1976–77 *Survey*. Special care was exercised to protect the confidentiality of the *Survey* responses to ensure complete and accurate results.

We hope that you will read the *Survey* results to see how your organization compares to those organizations responding to the *Survey*. We also hope you will give us your suggestions for improving next year's *Annual DP Training Survey* just as we will use the results to improve our services to you.

Thank you.

Results

1. What is your position or title? Check one. (98 responses)

	Number 1977	Percentage 1977	Percentage 1976
A. DP Training Director	53	54.1	54.3
B. DP Manager	14	14.3	4.3
C. Systems Manager	2	2.0	8.6
D. Operations Manager	0	0.0	0.0
E. Other	29	29.6	32.8
TOTAL	98	100.0	100.0

INTERPRETATION. Survey questionnaires were to be completed by "the individual who makes decisions or recommendations to acquire DP training for (their) organization." As in last year's survey results, a number of people in categories other than "DP Training Director" take an active role in this process. Many organizations of moderate size still do not have a designated DP Training Director. This year's *Survey* indicates more than ever that in many organizations, DP training decisions still remain with top DP management or their staff and support groups.

2. *If you are a DP Training Director, is DP training your full-time job? (51 responses)*

		Number	Percentage
A.	Yes	30	59
B.	No	21	41
	TOTAL	51	100

INTERPRETATION. Many DP Training Directors spend only part of their time on DP training. Their other duties include administration, standards and procedures (through the years, coupling training and standards has been a traditional favorite), and systems analyst work. Six respondents indicate that only a small part of their time is devoted to DP training. The DP Training Directors who do not spend full-time on DP training have an average annual DP training budget of $90,600. The average annual DP training budget of all respondents is $113,400. See *Survey* Question #8.

3. *How many full-time people make up your DP training staff? (95 responses)*

Average: 2.8 people
Range: 0 to 17 people

INTERPRETATION. See the Interpretation of *Survey* Question #4.

4. *How many of these full-time people report to you? (95 responses)*

Average: 1.7
Range: 0 to 17

INTERPRETATION. Full-time DP training staff members make up a small percentage of the overall DP organization's staff. The average respondent organization has 2.8 people working as full-time DP trainers while the average respondent DP organization has 273.8 people. (See Question #6.) This indicates that most responding organizations on the average have one full-time DP trainer for every 100 DP staff members. Of the 95 respondents to Questions #3 and #4, 29 indicated that their organizations have no full-time people on their DP training staffs. Twelve respondents are from organizations having at least five people on their DP training staffs headed by a designated DP Training Director. Question #4 indicates that the typical full-time DP training staff (when it exists) is made up of a DP Training Director having an average of 1.7 full-time DP trainers reporting to him or her.

5. *What is your annual salary? (89 responses made up of 50 DP Training Directors and 39 other titles)*

DP Training Directors (50)		All Respondents (89)	
Average:	$23,460	Average:	$23,100
Range:	$11,600 to	Range:	$11,600 to
	$40,000		$43,000

INTERPRETATION. The average annual salaries of DP Training Directors compares favorably with the annual average salaries of all respondents. The relatively high average salary for DP Training Directors indicates that top management places a high value on the DP Training Director function.

6. *How many people make up your entire DP organization? (94 responses)*

	Average 1977	Average 1976
A. DP Manager	28.2	28.9
B. Applications systems analysis and design	49.3	58.3

C. Applications
   programming   67.0   97.1
D. Systems (or   (not separated from
   operating systems)   Programming in
   programming   20.4   1976 Survey)
E. Operations   108.0   90.3
   TOTAL   273.8   274.6

INTERPRETATION. Like last year, respondent organizations are fairly large. Only six organizations having fewer than 50 people returned the completed questionnaire compared to 11 last year. The averages in all categories remain about the same between 1976 and 1977 results.

7. *What is your annual DP budget? (71 responses)*

Average: $7,600,000
Range: $1,400 to $35,000,000

INTERPRETATION. Like last year, organizations responding had, on the average, fairly sizeable DP budgets. However, a number of organizations reported very small DP budgets, for example, 10 organizations with budgets less than $1,000,000 returned questionnaires this year as compared to only five last year. The average annual DP budget this year is approximately $1,843,000 lower than last year's average.

8. *What is your annual DP training budget? (Count DP training staff salaries and overhead, but do not count course attendee salaries.) (85 responses)*

Average: $113,400
Range: $1,000 to $800,000

INTERPRETATION. The reported average DP training budget is still an incredibly low 1.5% of the reported average DP budget. (See Question #7.) However, this figure is slightly better than the 1.2% figure reported in last year's *Survey*.

9. How is your DP (training) budget distributed over these groups of people? (35 responses)

	Average
A. DP Management	$25,070
B. Applications systems analysis and design	23,290
C. Applications programming	46,410
D. System (or operating systems) programming	18,160
E. Operations	28,870
TOTAL	$141,800

INTERPRETATION. Comparing the average DP training budget by organizational group to the average number of people by organizational group (Question #6) yields some interesting figures. The average number of dollars spent annually for the following groups of people are shown below:

	1977	*1976*
DP Management	$889	$511
Applications Systems Analysis and Design	472	439
Applications Programming	683	606
System (or operating systems) Programming	890	(not included)
Operations	267	207
Staff and Support	(not included)	302
Average for Total DP Organization	$518	$340

DP Management and Programming increased significantly in average dollars spent while the Operations and Systems Analysis and Design remained about the same. Recent emphasis on programmer productivity and structured programming techniques has undoubtedly increased training in the programming area. Management category increases may reflect a burst of interest in distributed processing, privacy and security, long-range DP planning, and other hot management topics. Operations continues in its traditional role of receiving less training by a greater margin than the rest of DP.

Differences in Average for Total DP Organization between 1977 ($518) and 1976 ($340) could be explained by differences in people categories included in the questions for these years. There is also a discrepancy between the Average Total training budget reportedly distributed over these categories in Question #4 ($141,800) compared to the Average Total Annual DP Training Budget reported in Question #8 ($113,400). The difference in number of respondents to Questions #8 and #9 undoubtedly accounts for this discrepancy.

10. *Do you have a centralized DP training function or does every group within DP do its own training? (98 responses)*

	Number	Percentage
A. Centralized	81	82.7
B. De-Centralized	12	12.2
C. Both	5	5.1
TOTAL	98	100.0

INTERPRETATION. In recent years, the trend has been to centralize the DP training function and designate a person to direct the DP training activities. This could reflect a change in management attitude toward the value of training and its role in improving organizational effectiveness and profitability as organizations mature and become more stable.

11. *Is your DP training group a part of the DP department? (95 responses)*

	Number	Percentage
A. Yes	82	86.3
B. No	13	13.7
TOTAL	95	100.0

INTERPRETATION. Because of the specialized nature of DP training, the DP training function has traditionally been a part of the DP organization. As the need for formalizing DP career development and training programs becomes more evident, the influence of headquarters personnel and training organizations becomes more pronounced. This could lead to more DP training organizations becoming a part of such centralized administrative groups in the future.

12. How do you get your DP training budget? (98 responses)

	Number	Percentage
A. Operate on revolving fund and charge back course attendees.	8	8.2
B. Operate as overhead function as part of DP organization's budget.	74	75.6
C. Operate as overhead function as part of overall organization training (including non-DP)budget.	12	12.2
D. Other	3	3.0
B & C Above	1	1.0
TOTAL	98	100.0

INTERPRETATION. A large majority (87.8%) of DP training organizations are funded out of the overhead budgets of either the DP department or the non-DP training organization. This arrangement has sometimes caused instability for some DP training groups. During economic slowdowns, training as an overhead function is sometimes cut without warning. DP training organizations operating on a revolving fund basis are sometimes more secure from drastic cutbacks, because they can justify their existence in a pragmatic, bottom-line way. These revolving fund DP training organizations are more difficult to charter and organize, but often are more effective once they are established.

13. In what month do you prepare your budget? (96 responses)

Month Budget Preparation Started		Number	Percentage
January		5	5.2
February		2	2.1
March		3	3.1
April		1	1.0
May		3	3.1
June		4	4.2
July		6	6.3
August		8	8.3
September		20	20.8
October		29	30.2
November		12	12.6
December		3	3.1
	TOTAL	96	100.0

INTERPRETATION. Many organizations (19) indicated that their budget preparation activity spans more than one month. To simplify *Survey* result presentation, the month that respondents start their budget preparation is shown. Over 81% of the respondents start their budget preparation activity during the last six months of the calendar year. Over half of the respondents start their budget work during September and October.

14. What is the most serious problem you face in carrying out your DP training job? (94 responses)

The majority of the responses to this question fall into one of the following five problem categories:

A. Maintaining high-quality, up-to-date, and complete training programs (33 responses)

B. Lack of support from management (21 responses)
C. Time for training (13 responses)
D. Lack of a qualified training staff (13 responses)
E. Budget constraints—high cost of training (7 responses)

INTERPRETATION. Problem categories A and D reflect the recurring concern expressed by respondents to this *Survey* over the years, namely, the desire to ensure the quality of training presented to the DP staff members of respondent organizations. Problem categories B, C, and E reflect the long-standing conflict of priorities for management attention and organizational dollars. Fortunately, as reflected by this and past *Surveys*, this conflict appears to be resolving itself as the role of training in improving organizational effectiveness and profitability becomes more apparent to top management.

15. *For what course subject areas are you having difficulty in finding qualified outside vendor training? (82 responses)*

In tabulating responses to this question, the following course subject areas were identified as those for which respondents are having difficulty finding qualified outside vendor training:

A. Operations Training (9 responses)
B. Systems Analysis and Design (8 responses)
C. Data Base Design (5 responses)
D. Management (4 responses)
E. Data Communications (3 responses)
F. Hardware (3 responses)
G. Language Programming (3 responses)
H. Writing (3 responses)
I. Software Packages and Systems Programming (3 responses)
J. Structured Analysis, Design, and Programming (2 responses)
K. User Training (2 responses)
L. None (30 responses)

INTERPRETATION. Despite the apparent widespread availability of training on almost any DP subject, respondents are still concerned about finding *qualified* vendor training on a great range of subjects. The lack of good operator training (Problem Category A) has traditionally been a concern of DP trainers. The relatively small number of operations people to be trained and the highly specialized, configuration-dependence of the training contribute to the problem. Hardware vendors are most frequently the only source for operator training, and this source is often only marginally satisfactory. The lack of good systems analysis and design training (Problem Category B) often results from the difficulty in defining the needed skills and knowledge requirements in this area and then finding effective training methods to improve performance in these areas. This problem is shared by DP Training Directors and vendors alike.

16. *Do you send people to public vendor training courses? If not, why not? (98 responses)*

	Number	Percentage
A. Yes	88	89.8
B. No	10	10.2
TOTAL	98	100.0

INTERPRETATION. Most respondents utilize public vendor training courses. The main reason given for not sending people to public vendor training courses is budget constraints. The cost of public training courses will continue to rise and ultimately quality training vendors may not offer public training because of the high costs and risks of promoting public offerings.

17. *Do you use outside vendors to teach their courses at your offices? If not, why not? (98 responses)*

	Number	*Percentage*
A. Yes	77	78.6
B. No	21	21.4
TOTAL	98	100.0

INTERPRETATION. More people use vendor public training (see Question #16), than use vendor on-site training. Budgetary constraints and lack of enough people for vendor on-site training were the main reasons given to explain decisions not to use vendor on-site training. Most quality vendors offer their public courses for presentation on-site at client offices for eight to ten times the public registration fee.

18. *Do you train user department people? (97 responses)*

	Number	*Percentage*
A. No	27	27.8
B. Yes	70	72.2
TOTAL	97	100.0

INTERPRETATION. Of the 70 respondents who answered yes, 62 listed subjects that their user training covers. Over half of these respondents have introductory DP courses. Other subject areas mentioned include how to use application systems, project management, and systems analysis. Many organizations are taking advantage of the recent surge of user interest in DP training. They are providing user departments with DP training and using the proceeds to finance much needed DP department training which is more esoteric and more expensive.

19. *When your organization cuts its budget, how does training fare? (92 responses)*

	Responses	*Percentage 1977*	*Percentage 1976*
A. Training goes first.	14	15.2	14.5

B. Training goes second after_____.	1	1.1	1.5
C. Training is generally cut in proportion to the rest of the budget.	56	60.9	68.1
D. Training budget is generally not cut.	<u>21</u>	<u>22.8</u>	<u>15.9</u>
TOTALS	92	100.0	100.0

INTERPRETATION. Continued good news. Most organizations still report that training budgets fare as well as other organizational budgets when budget cut time comes. Although the percentage is down from last year's *Survey* results, more organizations still report that training budgets are "not generally cut" as report that training budgets are "the first to go" when overall budgets are cut. This was not true five years ago. Over the past five years, training has become recognized as an important hedge against the business conditions which result in reduced revenues and profits that often used to precipitate arbitrary and abrupt cuts in training budgets. This year's response might indicate that DP training budgets are leveling off and stabilizing.

> 20. *Where is your DP training budget headed? (97 responses)*

	Responses	Percentage 1977	Percentage 1976
A. Anticipate growth	58	59.8	71.4
B. Anticipate a cut	6	6.2	4.3
C. Status quo	<u>33</u>	<u>34.0</u>	<u>24.3</u>
TOTALS	97	100.0	100.0

INTERPRETATION. More good news. Almost without exception, respondents report anticipated growth or status quo in their training budget levels in the near future. This outlook is consistent with general economic conditions which bode well for the next 12–18 months. However, the percentage of organizations "anticipating growth" is lower than last year while the "status quo" percentage is up.

21. *Was your 1977 DP training budget increased over 1976 (not including general cost-of-living expenses)? (95 responses)*

		Responses	*Percentage*
A.	Increased more than cost of living	50	52.6
B.	Stayed about the same	40	42.1
C.	Decreased	5	5.3
	TOTAL	95	100.0

INTERPRETATION. The results of this question would tend to verify the traditional slow but steady growth of DP training budgets as organizations mature and stabilize. This is consistent with the results of Question #8 which showed a small increase of DP training budgets as a percentage of overall DP budgets.

22. *How many days of training each year does your DP training group provide each individual in these groups? (69 responses)*

	Average	*Cost Per Training Day*
A. People in DP management	6	$148.16
B. People in applications systems analysis and design	10.7	44.15

C. People in applications programming	14.2	48.13
D. People in systems (or operating systems) programming	8.9	100.02
E. People in operations	9.4	28.43

INTERPRETATION. By comparing the average number of dollars spent annually for each training group (see Question #9) with the average number of days of training provided each year, we were able to derive the cost per training day. Since people in DP management average only six days of training each year but spend $889 per person per year, their cost per training day is the highest. People in systems programming also have a high cost per training day since they average 8.9 days of training each year and spend $890.19 per person per year. People in operations have the lowest cost per training day, averaging 9.4 training days and spending $267.31.

23. Do you have a formal training program for systems analysts? (98 responses)

		Responses	Percentage
A.	No	44	44.9
B.	Yes	54	55.1
	TOTAL	98	100.0

If yes, how do you train the majority of your systems analysts?

		Responses	Percentages
A.	Internally developed and presented courses	10	18.5
B.	Audio-video training	11	20.5
C.	Outside vendor public training	6	11.1

D.	Outside vendor in-house training	4	7.4
E.	Other	3	5.6
F.	Combination of above	20	37.0
	TOTALS	54	100.0

INTERPRETATION. Developing an effective systems analysts training program appears to be one of the most difficult problems facing DP trainers today. Almost half of the 98 respondents have no formal systems analysts training program at all. Another 17 rely solely on audio-video training or vendor public training which, for most organizations, would normally represent only a partial solution to the problem. However, 20 respondents report using a combination of training approaches which, for them, indicates an effective balanced program focusing on this difficult training area. Another 10 respondents have their own courses in this area.

24. Has your organization implemented structured design and programming? (95 responses)

		Responses	Percentage
A.	No	34	35.8
B.	Yes	61	64.2
	TOTAL	95	100.0

If yes, how do you train the majority of your people in structured design and programming?

		Responses	Percentage
A.	Internally developed and presented courses	20	32.8
B.	Audio-video training	5	8.2

C.	Outside vendor		
	public training	3	4.9
D.	Outside vendor in-		
	house training	10	16.4
E.	Other	2	3.3
F.	Combination of		
	above	<u>21</u>	<u>34.4</u>
	TOTAL	61	100.0

INTERPRETATION. Most responding organizations have implemented structured design and programming and are using a mixture of training approaches to meet their training needs in this area. Of the 61 respondents who are training people in this subject area, 20 have their own courses on the subject and 21 more use a combination of training approaches to meet the training need. This would indicate a certain "maturity" of this subject area which would not have been so even two years ago.

25. *When making a decision between "making" and "buying" your own training programs, what is your primary consideration? Rank order from 1 (most important) to 4 (least important). (88 responses)*

Weighted Ranking

1. Number of students to be
   trained   2.02
2. Uniqueness of course   2.43
3. Reputation of vendor   2.71
4. Cost of vendor's training   2.79

INTERPRETATION. Respondents indicate that when making a decision between "making" or "buying" their own training programs, the number of students to be trained is the primary consideration. Cost of vendors training is the least important consideration. Predictably, uniqueness of course and vendor's reputation are frequently mentioned concerns that fall under the broad heading of course quality which this and past *Survey*s indicate as the major concern of DP trainers.

26. *List the outside training vendor you would first turn to for training on the following subjects. (Vendors receiving fewer than three first choice selections are not listed.) (84 responses)*

A. Beginning programming: Vendors (first choice selections)

1977 Survey Results	*1976 Survey Results*
Deltak (17)	IBM (15)
IBM (16)	ASI (9)
Local/In-house (14)	Deltak (8)
ASI (13)	Local/In-house (7)

B. Basic systems analysis: Vendors (first choice selections)

1977 Survey Results	*1976 Survey Results*
BSI (16)	IBM (10)
Deltak (15)	ASI (7)
ASI (12)	Deltak (7)
Systemation (7)	Systemation (4)
IBM (6)	Ware (4)
Yourdon (5)	BSI (4)
Ware (4)	ASM (3)
Local/In-house (4)	Colleges and Universities (3)

C. Basic systems design: Vendors (first choice selections)

1977 Survey Results	*1976 Survey Results*
Deltak (14)	IBM (9)
ASI (11)	ASI (7)
BSI (10)	Deltak (7)

Ware (5)   Yourdon (4)
Local/In-house (5)   BSI (4)
IBM (4)   ASM (3)

D. Structured design and programming: Vendors (first choice selections)

1977 Survey Results	*1976 Survey Results*
Yourdon (33)	Yourdon (23)
Deltak (13)	IBM (8)
BSI (12)	BSI (6)
ASI (8)	Deltak (6)

E. Data Base Design: Vendors (first choice selections)

1977 Survey Results	*1976 Survey Results*
IBM (19)	IBM (10)
Deltak (8)	Performance Development
ASI (7)	ment Corporation (5)
Local/In-house (5)	Deltak (4)
	Cullinane (3)

F. Operator Training: Vendors (first choice selections)

1977 Survey Results	*1976 Survey Results*
IBM (21)	IBM (18)
Deltak (20)	ASI (9)
ASI (15)	Deltak (6)
Local/In-house (6)	Hardware vendor (5)
	Local/In-house (3)

INTERPRETATION. Last year IBM was the most often selected first choice vendor in five out of six categories. This year, respondents chose IBM first in only two categories (Data Base Design and Operator Training). Deltak was also chosen first in two categories (Beginning Programming and Basic

Systems Design). BSI was the first choice vendor for Basic Systems Analysis, and Yourdon was again selected first for Structured Design and Programming.

Again this year, the answers to this question indicate a predilection to acquiring training from vendors who are "safe" or convenient (e.g., IBM) or who are simplest to justify in quantitative terms (audio-video training). While this question indicates which vendors respondents "first turn to for training," it may not necessarily indicate respondents' opinion of the vendor offering the "best buy." (See the results of Question #27.) Again this year, results of this question may be influenced by respondents who are smaller and less sophisticated and who spend less time and effort shopping for "training bargains" from smaller, high-quality vendors who are less well known than IBM and others.

27. *How would you rate the* cost *and* quality *of the training provided by the following vendors? Use this marking system. (92 responses)*

	Cost	Quality
4 — Exceptional	Very low	Exceptionally good
3 — Good	Low	Good quality
2 — Average	Average	Average
1 — Poor	High cost	Poor quality
0 — Don't know	—	—

Vendor	Cost (C)	Quality (Q)	C + Q	Ranking
AMA	1.87	1.80	3.67	14
AMR	1.88	2.29	4.17	11
ASI	2.21	2.60	4.81	4
Boeing Computer Service	1.82	2.76	4.58	6

BSI-Brandon	2.04	3.08	5.12	1
CDC-IAT	1.96	2.18	4.14	12
Deltak	2.02	2.69	4.71	5
Edutronics	2.39	1.88	4.27	9
Honeywell	2.00	2.18	4.18	10
IBM	1.69	2.83	4.52	7
Keane	1.55	2.44	3.99	13
Systemation	2.40	2.52	4.92	3
Ware	1.95	3.04	4.99	2
Yourdon	1.42	2.98	4.40	8

INTERPRETATION. Again this year, no vendor was rated better than Average to Good in the Cost category. The category that counts most, according to past and present *Survey* respondents, is quality. This year, only two vendors were given Quality ratings in the Good range (BSI and Ware). While a number of well-known vendors were given solid Poor ratings in the Cost category (including AMA, AMR, Boeing, IBM, and Yourdon), only two vendors were rated Poor in the Quality category (AMA and Edutronics). The Cost-plus-Quality (C + Q) Composite ranking indicates the "value" of training available from these vendors. Using the composite ranking of the 14 vendors, according to respondents, the "best buy" in DP training is available from BSI (1st), Ware (2nd), and Systemation (3rd) while the "worst buy" is available from CDC-IAT (12th), Keane (13th), and AMA (14th).

> *28. What additional questions should be asked on next year's ANNUAL DP TRAINING SURVEY? (34 responses)*

INTERPRETATION. Respondents have suggested some 34 additional questions for inclusion in next year's *Survey*. Certain questions in this year's *Survey* will be eliminated, modified, or expanded based on respondent comments.

29. Comments. (15 responses)

A number of suggestions were made to help respondents understand *Survey* questions more fully. These suggestions will be incorporated into next year's *Survey*. Additional suggestions are welcomed.

APPENDIX B

TIPS FOR TRAINERS: EXCERPTS FROM THE *BSI INSIDER NEWS*

(The *BSI Insider News* is published quarterly for the benefit of DP managers and training directors who are responsible for providing cost-effective training to their DP organization. The following TIPS for TRAINING are excerpts from recent issues of *Insider News* and will assist you in organizing an effective DP training program for your organization. You may subscribe to *Insider News* at no cost by contacting Brandon Systems Institute, Inc., 4720 Montgomery Lane, Bethesda, Maryland 20014, (301)986-8611.)

Contents

3. *Think Cost-per-Student-Day*
4. *Justifying the Training Budget—The Bottom Line*, by Nate A. Newkirk
5. *DP Personnel Skills Measurement Tools*
6. *Users Training—Source of your Budget*
7. *Evaluating Training Results—Theory and Practice*, by Nate A. Newkirk
8. *Solidify your Training Budget ... Tell Management How Good a Job You're Doing*
9. *What about Systems Analysis Training?*
10. BSI CONSORTIUM *Training Changed to Ease Invoicing and Collection*
11. *Schedule "Shoe-in" Courses Intuitively*
12. *An Action Program for Controlling Turnover*, by Nate A. Newkirk
13. Annual Survey *Proves Power of the Press Still a Force to Be Reckoned With*
14. *Programmer Aptitude Testing*
15. *DP Management Education*
16. *30 Training Ideas in 30 Minutes*
17. *CMI/CAI May Have Its Place in DP Training Too*
18. *Cost Justification and Making the Right DP Training Decisions*
19. *Making Performance Appraisal Programs Work*, by Nate A. Newkirk
20. *Can DP Training Solve the Turnover Problem?*
21. *Another Pitch for ASTD*
22. *Structured Human Resource Management System: A Total Solution for Organizations Committed to HRD for DP*
23. *Professionalism—The Most Essential Ingredient for a Successful DP Training Career*
24. *More on Programmer Aptitude Testing*
25. *Teaching Tips*
26. *Literature for DP Training Directors*
27. *New Literature*

1. The DP Trainer and the "Manhole Phenomenon"

DP trainers have traditionally suffered from the effects of what we at BSI call the "manhole phenomenon." We first observed this phenomenon a number of years ago and have done our very best to ease its negative impact ever since. What is this strange phenomenon?

First, most DP trainers are lone wolves in their DP organizations. So, they suffer from the acute affliction of not having anyone to talk to about their jobs. We dubbed this communication isolation the "manhole phenomenon." Why? Because DP trainers appeared to us like people working in manholes doing their job while completely isolated from the next DP trainer in another manhole only a few feet away. Both trainers were struggling with many of the same problems, building the same kind of training programs, and fighting the same frustrations.

We decided to do something about this terrible situation, and you're now reading the lastest BSI innovation designed to help DP trainers communicate more effectively. We hope you will help us by contributing to the *Insider News* your thoughts, news, and tips for other DP trainers. We'll continue to talk at user and professional groups to encourage CONSORTIUM training, to survey DP trainers annually and share the results with you, to act as an information exchange and referral service, and to expand our list of DP trainers all over the continent. You can also help by passing this newsletter along to your professional acquaintances who might benefit from a vicarious trip out of the manhole, courtesy of the *BSI Insider News*.

2. Reviewing Public Training Courses—Cheap Insurance

We highly recommend reviewing public presentations of a vendor's course before booking an in-house presentation of the course. Public reviewing lets you see the course materials and content firsthand and to review the classroom manner of a particular instructor. You can also meet with the instructor before and after class to discuss the ways that the course can be targetted to your organization. Most course instructors will gladly spend time with public course attendees who are seriously reviewing their course for in-house presentation. This face-to-face time together often ensures the success of a subsequent in-house presentation and builds rapport and understanding between you and the instructor.

If you can't review the course in public, at minimum check your instructor's references thoroughly. Be sure you are comfortable with your instructor's teaching style and knowledge of the subject before you accept your in-house instructor assignment. Finally, be sure to talk to the instructor at least a week before your in-house course to be sure that he knows what you want the course to achieve (objectives) and who will be in attendance (audience).

3. Think Cost-per-Student-Day

Always think in terms of cost-per-student-day. It's obvious that not all DP trainers do. You'd be amazed at the range of values that we received on our last DP training survey from our questions on DP trainers' expectations of the student-day costs for audio-visual training, vendor public training, and vendor in-house training. Remember that in-house vendor training may be your best training buy, providing the cost-per-student-day is not too high. We *know* that you can buy top-quality in-house vendor-provided, skill-oriented workshops, e.g., structured programming and design, systems analysis, and systems design, for well under $60 per student day. You shouldn't pay more unless your class size is unusually small.

4. Justifying the Training Budget—The Bottom Line, by Nate A. Newkirk

In 18 years of continuous involvement with DP and management training, I've found no subject so misunderstood or frustrating to my fellow training professionals as this one. So, when Gary Slaughter asked me to write this article, I was pleased to do so.

As is so popular with ad copy writers these days, the title of this article has a double meaning. Let's develop our reasoning around that idea—the bottom line. But first, some preparatory thoughts:

1. The approach to budgeting used by some TDs is to take last year's expense, add 10%, and plead eloquently. Quite a few TDs, recognizing the indefensibility of that approach *and*, having given themselves time to do so, ask their "users" to submit course plans for the coming year.

   The very few TDs who are blessed with a management which regards training as more than a necessary evil are going to be successful with either approach, while the rest look upon them enviously.

2. It is necessary for us to accept the idea that training is usually regarded by management as prime territory for budget cutting. After all, their logic goes, when times are tight everyone has to work harder because our staff is lean—there's less time for training.

3. Training, as you well know, is a staff function—which means that the TD can only advise, view with alarm, etc., but can't *decide* and *direct*.

4. When a manager is faced with the need (or the opportunity, for that matter) to cut *dollars* from the budget, he'll do it quickly and easily. But if the proposed cuts involve people, programs or projects, that's a lot tougher and less arbitrary.

5. No clear-thinking employee would refer to training as a company fringe benefit. They would describe it as the company's commitment to help them develop their capabilities to the fullest.

Now, let's see if we can put these 5 ideas together into something meaningful. Therefore:

1. Help your "user" managers to define skills deficiencies for each person and assign them priorities. Do likewise for career enhancement plans for the superior performers.
2. Present each manager a prioritized training plan for each individual, tied to the skills deficiencies or enhancements, and negotiate their commitment to release the individual for the required number of days.
3. Present your management with a two-part (deficiencies and enhancements) individualized, prioritized training plan showing dollars and staff days.
4. Always respond to suggestions (or edicts) for cuts by tying the cuts to the effect on your "user" manager's projects and people.

5. DP Personnel Skills Measurement Tools

From time to time, we are asked to recommend tools to help measure the skills levels of DP personnel. We know of a number of tools that are available to accomplish this. We hesitate to make a specific recommendation unless we have specific positive feedback from one of our client friends.

Part of our hesitation also stems from the recent court cases related to organizations using such skills measurement tools for selection and hiring. Some such tools have been found to be not properly validated and standardized and, therefore, in violation of equal rights laws, so be careful.

With all those caveats firmly in place, we bring one such tool to your attention. It is the Programmer Knowledge Survey (PKS) available from INSCO Systems Corporation in Neptune, New Jersey, [(201) 922-1100]. One of our client friends has recently used the PKS and reports good results in the skills analysis project that he has just completed. The PKS approach allows testing to be done by a CRT terminal connected to INSCO's computer. The test is then scored automatically and the individual's score is summarized in comparison to others at the individual's experience level. Other services are provided as well.

(The May 1976 issue of *Infosystems* magazine featured an article on PKS entitled, "Lowering Programmer Turnover Rate." Reprints of the article are also available from INSCO Systems.)

6. Users Training—Source of your Budget

The source of budgeting of many a healthy training organization comes from an unusual place . . . a place that many DP training directors don't like to reveal openly. The place is the user departments. Smart DP training directors who want to support a well-rounded and technically up-to-date training program can seek out this hungry audience for their courses. It's only natural. User departments are beginning to originate the demand for training in subjects like distributed processing, computer security, fundamentals of computers, and systems analysis. Taking advantage of the natural trend toward widening user department requirements might be just the key to spreading the budgetary risks of your DP training program, building a much broader following throughout your organization, and winning the amazed support of top DP management in the process. Why should DP management be pleased? Wouldn't you be happy if your DP training director was able to configure his training program so the user departments, not DP, paid for all the esoteric training that you need to keep your DP staff happy and competent?

7. Evaluating Training Results—Theory and Practice, by Nate A. Newkirk

THEORY   Can you imagine a conversation like this?

Tom: I'm going on a trip.
Dick: Where to?
Tom: I don't know.
Dick: How will you know when you get there?
Tom: Huh?

Training is a "trip." The destination? A more productive employee. Therefore, define "more productive" and "employee" carefully, and you're ready to map your course.

Need we say more? Unfortunately, yes.

First, that theory you just read is sound. There's no denying it. And you must understand it thoroughly.

Second, the prime roadblock to its use is your understanding of its application in a real world.

MORE THEORY   A staff person's job (TDs included) involves *helping* meet the needs of the group being served. It also involves *assuring* cost-effective use of that help. The staffer, unfortunately, can only recommend.

PRACTICE   The key to a TD's success is *frequent* face-to-face contact with his/her "users." That requires:

1. Having a *reason* for the contact
2. A *willingness* by both to have the contact

If the result of this contact is better help to the user, it will continue.

Step 1: *Every* training request deserves a chat with the student's boss. Focus the discussion on results to be expected and the student's background. Describe results as "what the student can do now."

Step 2: Follow that up with a note, describing results of the meeting, and your recommendations. Include your plans to evaluate results, which usually should not be done until several weeks after training.

Step 3: Deliver that note personally. Answer questions. Gain concurrence. Get a commitment that the student will attend the course. Inform boss and student how student evaluation will occur in the course (it *will*, won't it?).

Step 4: At course end, give a verbal student evaluation to student and boss. It should focus on the student's ability to carry out new tasks, backed up with specifics on student's *performance* in class. No unrelated attitudinal or behavior comments are appropriate.

Step 5: When post-training evaluation time arrives, interview both student and boss. Get input on current performance and on the good and bad parts of the training.

Step 6: Document the information you received *on the training*, add your plan for correcting problems, and send a copy to student and boss.

Step 7: Follow up with the trainer to assure that adjustments are made to the course.

(If you recall my article in the last issue, you'll realize that the process just described somewhat parallels that described to prepare a training budget. Why not? That is a *planned, scheduled* activity, while this is a response to unplanned needs.)

MORE PRACTICE TDs must spend time with managers whom they serve. Start each conversation with the question, "What's the biggest problem that you have in terms of your people's inability to do their jobs adequately?"

Focus on productivity and your role in helping achieve it, and managers will welcome you.

8. Solidify your Training Budget ...
Tell Management How Good a Job You're Doing

We reiterated the necessity to let management know just how much, how well, and what you are doing for them in the DP training area at least once a year. Our friend John Rose, DP training director at PPG Industries in Pittsburgh, has made management year-end reporting an integral part of his way of doing business. John has perhaps one of the most elaborate and successful DP training programs that we know of. His program is a mix of PPG developed and presented courses, audio-video courses integrated with instructor monitors for interactive assistance to students, and outside vendor training in the CONSORTIUM format shared with other members of the Pittsburgh Chapter of the ASTD EDP Special Interest Group.

John's program is given full blessing by PPG top management in part because, at the end of each calendar year, John prepares a comprehensive report to management that frankly tells management all he has done for them and their company over the year. We recommend that each DP training director do the same, whether your management asks for it or not. January 1977's training accomplishments highlight all the courses presented, the number of enrollees, the cost of the training, the number of days training per student, the fees saved by attending John's and CONSORTIUM courses rather than outside courses, and so on. John even lists all the outside courses attended by PPG employees and spells out their costs to show the comparison.

We think John has provided us with a good example of

what every DP training director should be doing at a minimum. If you would like a free copy of John's six-page year-end report, as a model for your year-end report, just return the enclosed information request card.

9. What about Systems Analysis Training?

Nearly half the 98 organizations responding to the recent *BSI Annual DP Training Survey* reported that they had no formal training program for systems analysts. Frankly, this shocked us, because we consider systems analysis to be one of the most important functions performed in the systems development process. After all, what is the alternative to good systems analysis? One alternative is a beautifully designed, structured system that is reliable, maintainable, and perfectly documented ... but a system that users can't use because it doesn't meet their needs.

We think there are at least two principal reasons why systems analysis training is one of the "last frontiers" in DP training. First, these critical systems analysis skills relating to the user-DP interface are skills in the behavioral or human communication category. They are intangible skills as opposed to the quantitative and technical skills that DP professionals feel comfortable with. We are naturally intimidated by these intangible skills because we can't identify, quantify, and measure them. Second, "systems analysis" means so many things to so many people. According to a recent study, a group of people described over 300 functions that they thought made up what is called "systems analysis."

At a recent GUIDE meeting, BSI president, Gary Slaughter, presented a model for DP trainers to structure their thinking about the systems analysis function and about the skills and knowledge requirements needed to support the functional areas included in the common definition of systems analysis. He presented two approaches to establish a systems analysis training program including specific recommendations for courses to make up the systems analysis training program.

At a full-day seminar on how to develop a systems analysis training program sponsored by the Pittsburgh ASM Chapter, BSI vice-president, Ben Knowles, covered some of the same ground, but Ben also added his thoughts on how a systems analysis training program would differ from organization to organization depending on the level of maturity and formalization of that organization. Ben Knowles is the BSI curriculum manager and principal developer of BSI's new, successful *Systems Analysis Workshop* (SAW).

If you are just thinking about a systems analysis training program, call BSI. We may have some advice that will save you steps.

10. BSI CONSORTIUM Training Changed to Ease Invoicing and Collection

BSI has had a successful record of helping over 50 organizations over the past three years to sponsor and conduct CONSORTIUM training in their local DP communities. As attractive as CONSORTIUM training is to individual organizations and groups, there is a reluctance on the part of some organizations to become involved in the invoicing and collection of course fees from outsiders. Breaking with past tradition, BSI recently agreed to invoice and collect the pro rated costs of an in-house *Systems Analysis Workshop* (SAW) among all attendees of a special CONSORTIUM sponsored through the Chicago DP Education Council (CDPEC). The March CONSORTIUM was attended by 25 students (with 10 students on the waiting list in case of cancellations). The result was the delivery of the top-quality BSI SAW to CONSORTIUM participants at about one-third the training cost and without any out-of-town travel costs. Needless to say, the experiment was a smashing success.

Since the Chicago success, the idea has caught on and similar pro rata sharing CONSORTIUM offerings are now confirmed for Philadelphia and Albuquerque. For more details, contact BSI.

Incidentally, if you have a local group of DP professionals or DP trainers, a BSI officer might be willing to visit your meeting at no cost to your group to explain the benefit of the CONSORTIUM approach as BSI has done in Washington, New York, Chicago, Pittsburgh, and Denver.

If you missed our recent announcement of organizations that are sponsoring BSI CONSORTIUM Training across the country, see the enclosed press release.

11. Schedule "Shoe-in" Courses Intuitively

Many DP training directors, especially new ones, spend too much time surveying their constituents to determine the interest, need, and timing for vendor in-house training courses. This time-consuming surveying activity often has these results: (1) delayed training even if the training is needed; (2) constituents making commitments to enroll their people, then later breaking their commitments; (3) constituents not answering the survey at all; (4) constituents telling you that they have ten people, when they really only have five people; (5) constituents telling you that they have ten people when they really have 20 people; or (6) by the time you receive the results of the survey, people have transferred, the training has increased in price, or higher priority training or other projects have intervened and you must repeat the survey the following January. Sound familiar?

Our tip is this. If you intuitively know that the course under consideration is one that your organization can use or if you have a formal DP career structures and development plan that allows you to know absolutely that your organization can use it, then schedule it. Tell your constituents that the course will be held, so come on and sign up now ... first come, first served. Most vendors *should* understand that, if your constituents do not support the course to a level that makes the course economically viable, you may have to cancel the tentative booking. (Be sure the vendor knows ahead of time that this is what you're doing.) If you are talking to a vendor who will not support this tentative booking approach to save you from that time-consuming surveying job, maybe you should consider looking for another vendor.

12. An Action Program for Controlling Turnover, by Nate A. Newkirk

It seems that everywhere I go I find different attitudes about turnover. In some places the mention of the word hardly causes a raised eyebrow. In other places it may trigger an "expletive deleted."

First, let's define terms. *Turnover*—persons who leave because they were discharged or they resigned. (Since you can't control employee deaths or retirement, why include them?) *Rate*—an annual percentage.

Few organizations would be comfortable if they had a turnover rate of 30% in their DP professional staff. But a turnover rate of 5% or less may be equally unhealthy. Further, once you've determined what your turnover rate is, so what?

Let's state 6 important concepts, then describe the action program.

1. Controlling turnover is a "womb-to-womb" proposition. It starts as soon as someone is hired, and continues until 2 or 3 months after he/she leaves. There's seldom one thing that makes the difference. It's a lot of things.

2. The objective is to improve the quality of your work force. "Turnover rate" must not address strictly quantity. Are you losing good people for good reasons? Good people for bad reasons? Some turnovers are more acceptable than others.

3. Some turnovers are reluctant to state the real reasons. They don't want to burn their bridges. Further, at the time they leave, they may not be clear in their own minds about what their reasons are. They may also later come to realize they've made a mistake. If they feel they're welcome, they may ask for their old job back.

4. Some managers may not want the truth known about why they have turnovers in their group. After all, managers are human, too. They make mistakes.

5. You can't compare apples and oranges. All companies don't calculate their turnover rate the same way. Anyway, your company *is* different. The idea is to improve *your* turnover rate, not just make it better than someone else's. Don't be like the statistician who drowned in a lake which had an average depth of two feet.

6. Your company's performance rating procedure should identify the *few* people who are superior, the *few* people who are unsatisfactory, the average performers, and those who are above average and below average. The simple fact is that we care more about keeping some employees than others.

ACTION PROGRAM

1. Set up your record-keeping system. Track turnover by performance rating, by functional groups (professional, technical, managerial, administrative), and by department (what managers are better than others). Monitor length of service, amount of training received, employment source (agency, college hire, employee referral), employee's reason for leaving, average time between promotions, and average annual salary increase.

Going back two or three years, collect and analyze as much of the above information as you can for each turnover. Be sure your paper work makes it easy to collect these data for all future turnover.

2. Set up some goals that you'd like to achieve for each of the five categories of performers. For example, the turnover rate should be dropping for superior performers, rising for unsatisfactory performers. The average seniority of superior turnovers should be rising, for unsatisfactories it should be dropping. Then track progress continuously, and report results, adjusting policies as results dictate.

3. Institute procedures which spot hiring errors early. For example, the first performance appraisal should be not later than three months after hiring, the next one six months later. Initial training should also be used as evaluation. The hiring process is still a crap game. No one has foolproof hiring methods. Identify mistakes early and correct them early.

4. It's a few really good ones that you *especially* don't want to lose. Institute special programs for them. Sure, their pay should increase more rapidly, but there's more. Superior performers learn quickly and become bored quickly. Then their performance falls off, and they tend to seek more challenging work (elsewhere?). Superior performers should not remain in a given assignment for more than 12 to 18 months. New assignments must be more challenging, more complex, more important. Therefore, they should receive more training than those whose careers are not advancing as rapidly.

5. *Never* hire an outsider to fill a job above entry level unless *all* managers agree that no one inside is capable. Promotion from within is a must.

6. Measure all manager's performance on their success in promoting and transferring. Give them "F" whenever they

say, "that person is too critical to release." No one is indispensable.

7. Your performance appraisal procedures should include documenting data on employee potential and a program for using that data to plan promotions and transfers. It should also include a document which employees fill out, allowing them to comment on the company, the management, their job, and their ambitions. This document should also be input to the planning process.

8. Money is not a good form of *public* recognition. Other programs are necessary for that. The idea is to be sure that people who do extra good jobs are publicly recognized. Be creative, be liberal, and be *fair.*

9. Tell superior performers what's in store for them in the next year or two—money, title, recognition, *especially,* the work that they'll be doing and the training they'll receive. The better and more ambitious the employee, the more important this is. (If you do this when trying to *hire* a good person, and I'll bet you sometimes do, why not when trying to *keep* someone?)

10. When a turnover occurs, put the person in one of two categories: (A) we really, really want him/her back, or (B) we don't care that much. Assign someone to keep in touch with each "A." Send them the department newsletter. Let them know they are missed. One day they might decide the grass isn't greener. Make sure they know they're welcome back.

11. Two or three months after a turnover leaves, have the confidential exit interview done by someone outside the department. The turnover will then be more willing to talk, and unimportant reasons will have faded away.

Are these programs easy? No way. Are they all possible and practical? Sure. There's not one untried idea in the whole program. The question is, How many must you institute? Your turnover analysis will answer that. The rest is up to management.

13. Annual Survey Proves Power of the Press Still a Force to Be Reckoned With

In an issue of *Infosystems* magazine the *BSI Annual DP Training Survey* was described and editorialized at length. The magazine article's last paragraph concluded with an offer to readers to check the box on the enclosed "bingo cards" and return it to *Infosystems* for a free copy of the *Annual Survey*. So far, *Infosystems* has forwarded BSI 250 requests for copies of the *BSI Annual DP Training Survey*. This just goes to show you that people are still very interested in what the other guy is doing in the area of DP training. We at BSI hope that we are helping to close this communication gap among DP training directors with such services to the DP industry as our *Survey* and this *Insider News*. And we'll do it with the help of our friends from the press!

14. Programmer Aptitude Testing

At a recent gathering of DP training directors, we polled the group to see what success people were having in using available programmer aptitude tests. We were surprised at the almost unanimous high regard for the SRA Computer Programmer Aptitude Battery. We requested information about the battery from SRA and were pleased to receive copies of the complete Test, Score Sheet, and an Examiner's Manual. To request your copy contact:

> Science Research Associates, Inc.
> 259 East Erie Street
> Chicago, Illinois 60611

SRA did not charge us anything for our set of materials.

15. DP Management Education

At the ASTD National Conference in Chicago, Roger Sullivan presented a 15-page overview of DP management training. During his presentation Roger spent some time explaining how the DP environments' unique aspects result in a unique problem for management trainers. He also details the why, what, and how of DP management education. Roger's wealth of personal experience in DP training is reflected in the paper. If you are interested in a copy of his book on the subject of DP training, contact him at the address below:

> Mr. Roger Sullivan
> Director of Education-MIS
> Commercial Union Companies
> One Beacon Street
> Boston, Massachusetts 02108

16. 30 Training Ideas in 30 Minutes

We've never consciously given a competitor an outright endorsement, but we think that we can break our rule just this once. The lucky vendor is ICS, an employee and management development company headquartered in Scranton, Pennsylvania. ICS has produced a Showcase Session for the ASTD National Conference entitled "30 Training Ideas in 30 Minutes." It was excellent. The Showcase session presented a panel of six training directors from business who discussed five training techniques that he/she considered to be particularly effective.

We were lucky enough to sit through the Showcase Session. If you didn't make it, you can still request your copy of the neat little brochure that ICS has published to describe the 30 ideas in some detail. Just call them at (717) 342-7701, ext. 317.

17. CMI/CAI May Have Its Place in DP Training, Too

We have resisted the temptation to proliferate the word of CMI and CAI, because, like other forms of non-live-instructor training, its advocates seem to behave as if CMI/CAI is the total solution to *everyone's* training problem. Of course, that's simply not true.

However, we are now convinced that training of users in certain applications areas can be effectively accomplished using CMI/CAI. And we have to be particularly impressed by the PLATO system, marketed by yet another BSI competitor, Control Data Education Company. PLATO appears to be an excellent training resource for organizations who can afford it. PLATO can be used for teaching new skills and procedures, simulation of highly technical situations, and introducing new systems to a wide audience of terminal users.

We were impressed by the detailed nature of the marketing documentation provided at no cost by John Lacey, President, Control Data Education Company. If you're interested in learning what PLATO could offer you, call John Lacey's office at (612) 853-5355.

18. Cost Justification and Making the Right DP Training Decisions

We have discovered another excellent source of information concerning cost justification and selection of the appropriate DP training alternative. Steve Comstock is an independent computer training and career development consultant, based in Denver, Colorado. Steve has assisted a number of BSI client friends and comes highly recommended.

Steve has published a white paper consisting of several chapters all related to the question of selecting and cost justifying the "right" DP training alternative for your people.

Steve has agreed to make this 35-page paper available to you at no cost if you simply call him at (303) 355-2752. By the way, the title of Steve's paper is "An Analysis of Alternatives in Data Processing Training." It's BSI recommended reading.

19. *Making Performance Appraisal Programs Work,* by Nate A. Newkirk

THE MACHIAVELLI TOUCH Given the assignment to install a Performance Appraisal and Counseling Program in a company, and given his understanding of human nature, here might be Niccolo Machiavelli's first directive to management:

On each employee's anniversary date, the employee is to be given an overall performance rating of one of the following five categories:

A. Superior
B. Above Average
C. Satisfactory
D. Minimum Satisfactory
E. Unsatisfactory

This rating will be assigned by the employee's immediate superior. The employee will be required to sign the rating form (and may add comments as desired), as will the rating manager.

Then the famous strategist would sit back and watch. His thought, of course, is that the program might require some "enhancements." However, he says to himself, these must arise out of a need identified after its implementation.

Situation 1: Penelope is appraised on July 1, and on July 2 a new manager comes in to replace her previous manager. Penelope, reasonably content with yesterday's appraisal, says to Machiavelli, "Does this mean I must wait 364 days to find out what my new manager *really* thinks of me?" Machiavelli sympathetically responds, "Of course not. We'll vary the time between appraisals as a function of how long you've worked for a given manager."

Situation 2: Ezekiel is appraised on August 1, and on August 2 is promoted to a higher, more complex position still reporting to the same manager. Ezekiel, pleased with yesterday's appraisal, says to Machiavelli, "Does this mean I must wait 364 days to find out how my manager appraises my work in my newer, tougher position?" Machiavelli replies, "We'll also vary the time as a function of your tenure in your current assignment."

Situation 3: Henrietta, confident of her ability, is surprised when her boss rates her "Satisfactory." She says to Machiavelli, "I know why. Last month I beat my boss at quoits 3 times. He's getting his revenge." Machiavelli consoles, "We'll require your boss's boss to sign his approval before you must sign."

Situation 4: Arthur, an egotist if he's anything, comes complaining. "My boss rated me only 'Above Average.' I know he rated 5 out of his 10 people 'Superior.' He's arbitrary and capricious." Machiavelli pauses. At last he arrives at a solution. We'll establish a distribution pattern for the five levels, then evaluate the program by checking to see if our employees are rated according to that pattern."

As you can see, Machiavelli's scheme is starting to work. Why? *Because he's listening to the employees.*

20. Can DP Training Solve the Turnover Problem?

In an issue of *Insider News*, we were fortunate to have two pieces of good news in the area of turnover control. First was Nate Newkirk's fine article, "An Action Program for Controlling Turnover," and second was our promise that, in the next issue, we would feature the results of an important study in this area conducted by one of our client friends. The study results are now available. Here is the author's abstract of his study report.

Can training affect turnover? A case study conducted in a 600-employee software development organization shows that it can.

The study showed that the turnover rate for employees participating in training and development was 10%, versus a 45% turnover rate for those employees not participating. Regarding dollars expended for training and development, the study also showed that 92% of the dollars expended were retained in the company, while only 8% were lost through termination.

If this isn't justification enough, a model for justifying the cost of training is presented. Basically, the model says that since the turnover rate for training participants is lower than that for nonparticipants, if the total number of employees participating is increased, a drop in the termination should result.

The key to making effective use of results like those above starts with precise documentation. The study makes suggestions for various types of data to be kept and provides an example of the uselessness of inaccurate and incomplete data.

If you are interested in receiving the entire turnover study report, request your copy by returning the enclosed card. We'll send you one without charge. (Don't forget that you may not be able to use the author's results, but his approach and advice on how to do your study are invaluable.)

21. Another Pitch for ASTD

ASTD membership can make a *good* DP trainer an *excellent* DP training professional by providing the following important benefits:

Subscription to the *Training and Development Journal*, ASTD's monthly magazine.

Listing in and your own copy of the annual, *Who's Who in Training and Development*, the ASTD membership directory

The *National Report for Training and Development* and the *Consultant Directory and Buyer's Guide*

Access to the Member Inquiry Service (to get free answers to your every training question) and Position Referral Service (to get a lead on your next job)

Member discounts on the excellent ASTD books, cassettes, and other professional services

An invitation to attend the next National ASTD Conference

No DP training director should be without a membership in this beneficial organization. For membership information, contact ASTD directly at (608) 274-3705. We hope you will join ASTD for professionalism.

22. Structured Human Resource Management System: A Total Solution for Organizations Committed to HRD for DP

Manufacturers Hanover Trust Company (MHT) has recently made available for purchase by other DP organizations its total, comprehensive HRD system for DP called "Structured Human Resource System." We have been told that this system is excellent for organizations with a large DP department and a strong commitment to do the HRD job right. MHT has just installed the system at the Federal Reserve Bank of New York, and the initial results are impressive.

The system encompasses standard approaches and tools to meet your DP organization's needs in the following areas:

Organizational planning and staffing

Job descriptions and career path structures

Skills definition and matrixing

Performance evaluation, objective setting, and potential rating

Career counseling and planning

We're not sure what this packaged system sells for, but we know that customized versions of such a comprehensive system could cost up to $200,000. For a free brochure on the system, call Dave LaBelle at MHT at (212) 623-5662.

23. *Professionalism—The Most Essential Ingredient for a Successful DP Training Career*

As we roam the country speaking before groups of DP managers and training directors, we emphasize the critical need for building professionalism in DP training. DP trainers traditionally know much more about "DP" than they do about "training." This phenomenon is understandable, but not commendable. Therefore, we do everything in our power to help DP training directors increase and improve their professionalism.

If you believe your own propaganda, you believe, as we do, that training is a good way to build professionalism. We believe strongly that every DP training director at minimum should attend three courses to help them do a more professional job: (1) a course on human resource development programs for DP (naturally, we recommend Nate Newkirk's HRD course); (2) a course on administering the DP training function (the Deltak ECW course is a good one); and (3) a train-the-trainer course addressing training techniques. This last category of course is a tough one to find, but we have assembled a few choices for you. Recently, we received public course announcements for the following training techniques courses. Contact these training suppliers directly for information:

Course Title	Training Supplier	Telephone
Managing the Training Function	Applied Management Institute Woodland Hills, California	(213) 348-9101
Effective Classroom Instruction	Applied Management Institute Woodland Hills, California	(213) 348-9101
Train-the-Trainer Series	ASTD Washington Chapter	(202) 659-9187
The Training Function	American Society for Training and Development Madison, Wisconsin	(604) 274-3440
Designing Effective Training and Selecting Appropriate Methods	American Society for Training and Development	(604) 274-3440
Teaching Techniques for the Instructor/ Trainer	The University of Chicago	(212) 953-7262
Platform Skills and Techniques	American Management Association New York, New York	(212) 246-0800

We will keep you advised of other course offerings that will help you to build your training professionalism.

24. More on Programmer Aptitude Testing

The terrible turnover problem in today's DP industry has caused many of our client friends to initiate their own entry-level training program for programmers. One of the toughest aspects of establishing a homegrown programmer training program is the problem of candidate selection. This problem has been recognized by a number of suppliers of programmer aptitude tests. There is one test, however, that has stood the test of time, so we thought our readers should know about it—The Wolfe Computer Aptitude Test.

We once used the test ourselves when we were in the software development business. As a matter of fact, our publishing division was the sole supplier of the test to the U.S. during the late 1960s. While we no longer use the test, our British affiliate, BIS Applied Systems, has continued in the software business and also has continued using the test. Since first used by BIS, the test has been administered to over 12,000 BIS employees and client employees in the UK. Some 300 BIS companies have used the Wolfe test.

The Wolfe test has been validated, which is important for EEO considerations. The tests are given at your offices and then scored and evaluated by Wolfe at their offices. The testing may be done for as little as $30 per person if you have a sufficient number of candidates. A detailed report on candidate ability is provided by Wolfe.

For more information, don't contact us, but call or write:

Wolfe Computer Aptitude Testing, Ltd.
P.O. Box 1104
St. Laurent Station
Montreal, Canada H4L 4W6

Wolfe also has aptitude tests for systems analysts and systems programmers.

25. Teaching Tips

The June 1978 issue of *Training HRD* contained an excellent article entitled "Tips for Teaching." The article featured tips prepared by Larry G. McDougle from the University of Indiana. For those of you who don't subscribe, here are the first nine of the 19 tips that Larry provides us.

1. Education is a joint enterprise: Students learn best when they contribute to the educational process.
2. As an instructor, you can be wrong at times, so admit mistakes. And don't bluff if you don't know.
3. When preparing to teach a course, clearly define the course objectives, and select a text that teaches techniques, materials, and assignments to best meet those objectives.
4. In determining assignments, plan the course in its entirety and allocate sufficient time to cover the various topics. Plan for holidays, examinations, review, etc.
5. Remember: Most students want you to "take charge." They want to feel they are being allowed to contribute, but, at the same time, they expect the instructor to provide direction.
6. When you meet a class for the first time, clearly define the classroom structure, i.e., let the students know from the outset exactly what is expected of them and what they can expect from you. Introduce yourself to the class and say something about your background and qualifications. Distribute a course outline and schedule—and go over them carefully to give your students an overview of the course.
7. The course outline should contain: (a) name of course, time and place it meets; (b) name of instructor and how he or she may be reached; (c) list of course objectives; (d) title of textbook; (e) assignments; (f) course requirements; (g) dates for examinations; (h) policy on grading/attendance/class participation; (i) resources available, e.g., books on reserve in library, audio-visual materials, etc.

8. When organizing a classroom presentation, try the "sandwich method"—tell students what you are going to tell them, tell them what you have told them. Studies reveal that most students want the instructor to draw appropriate conclusions rather than leaving the conclusions strictly to them.

9. Avoid *personal* criticism of a student when opposing his or her opinion or position on a given issue. Attack the argument, if necessary, *not* the student.

26. Literature for DP Training Directors

Several new publications for DP trainers have come to our attention. Each publication is described briefly below with the publisher's address and phone number where available. Contact the publisher directly for further information about the publication:

Government Training News. A monthly newsletter for government training directors with helpful information for even nongovernment trainers. Cost is $72 per year. Contact: Carnegie Press, Hillcrest Road, Madison, New Jersey 07940.

EDP Training News. A monthly newsletter especially for DP trainers. This publication is new, so we reserve judgment on its value. The first issue contained enough useful information for DP trainers to urge us to recommend it to our readers. Cost is $72 per year. Published by the same people who publish *Government Training News.* (See address above.)

Audio-Visual Source Directory. A semi-annual directory of A-V services and products, useful for outfitting and maintaining an A-V training center. Cost is not known. Contact: National Audio-Visual Association, Inc., 3150 Spring Street, Fairfax, Virginia 22031.

Training and Development Organizations Directory. Described by its publisher as a 614-page reference work describing firms, institutes, and other agencies offering training programs for business, industry, and government. Cost is $45. Contact: Gale Research Company, Book Tower, Detroit, Michigan 48226.

Seminars. Published three times a year as an aid to trainers trying to identify public training course offerings in a wide range of subject areas. Cost is $25 per year. Contact: Seminar Locater, Langdon Hall, 525 North Lake Street, Madison, Wisconsin 53703, (608) 251-2421.

Illustrated Trade References, Audio-Visual Equipment Volume. Yet another catalog of A-V equipment for trainers outfitting a training center. Cost is $10 per copy. Contact: Bill Daniels Co., Inc., Markade Building, 6750 West 75th Street, Post Office Box 2056, Shawnee Mission, Kansas 66201, (913) 831-0098.

Training World. A monthly magazine for training professionals. The magazine was originally called *Sales Training*, but, in an attempt to make the magazine more appealing to a general training audience, the publisher changed the name and added articles of a general nature. The magazine is not general enough for our taste yet, but it's progressing nicely. Cost is $8.50 per year. Contact: *Training World*, Suite 1026, 60 East 42nd Street, New York, New York 10017.

Bulletin on Training, published every two months by BNA Communications, Inc., Rockville, Maryland 20850, (301) 948-0540. Each issue features an interview with a prominent DP or training personality (e.g., Peter Drucker and Isaac Auerbach) and several other small articles providing useful hints for trainers. For example, the July/August 1977 issue contains a "checklist article" entitled "Handouts—Help, Hindrance or Happenstance." This might be a good issue to ask to see as a free sample if BNA will honor such a request. Cost is

$18.00 per year. Contact: BNA Communications Inc., 9401 Devonverly Hall Road, Rockville, Maryland 20850.

Directory of Management Education Programs, published by American Management Associations and offered through ASTD for a special price of $105.00 reduced from the normal price for non-ASTD members of $125.00. If you are an ASTD member, call ASTD at (608) 274-3705. If you are not an ASTD member call AMA at (212) 246-0800. This publication seems to contain every known management course available anywhere.

27. New Literature

Here's some new and some not-so-new literature that is available to help DP trainers do their jobs:

Training and Development Handbook, sponsored by ASTD and edited by Robert L. Craig, McGraw-Hill Book Company, New York, $26.50 (discount if ordered by ASTD members through ASTD), 866 pages.

This is a *must* book for any DP trainer's library. Complete, practical, and informative.

Written Communication for Data Processing, Randi Sigmund Smith, Van Nostrand Reinhold Company, New York, $12.95, 194 pages.

This is the text for the BSI *Effective Written Communication in DP Workshop*. Practical and fun book to read and learn from.

The Source Data Compendia (150 pages), published by *The Journal*, Technological Horizons in Education, P.O. Box 992, Anton, Massachusetts 01720, (617) 263-3607. Price: $15.00. This publication "combines products and services of all known manufacturers in five vital industries (computers and peripherals, A/V and multi-media, video, micrographics, and administrative and office equipment) serving the education field." Advertisers pay to list in this publication, so be wary. You may want to inspect this publication before you buy it.

The Oravisual Product Catalog #17. A complete catalog of Oravisual audio and visual communication products. Write to:

Oravisual Company, Inc.
Box 1150
St. Petersburg, Florida 33733

Books 1978. A complete listing of the newest ASTD books. Write to:

American Society for Training and Development
P.O. Box 5307
Madison, Wisconsin 53705

AMA's Directory of Management Education Programs. Two volumes of academic and nonacademic training courses for managers. Available through AMA or through ASTD (for member discount). Join ASTD and acquire this publication at the same time. Write to:

American Society for Training and Development
P.O. Box 5307
Madison, Wisconsin 53705

Management Development Course Catalog from the Management Institute, University of Wisconsin-Extension. A comprehensive program of training courses on all subjects for managers. Write to:

Department of Business and Management
University of Wisconsin-Extension
432 North Lake Street
Madison, Wisconsin 53700

Training Needs Assessment: A Study of the Methods, Approaches, and Procedures Used by Government Agencies. A good description of a needs assessment approach. Write to:

Mr. Thomas DeLauro, Jr.
Regional Training Consultant
U.S. Civil Service Commission
Federal Building
600 Arch Street
Philadelphia, PA 19106

Keep current, read DP training professional literature.

Appendix C

How to Organize a DP Training Directors Group in Your DP Community

Those of you who know me from various meetings that we have attended, know that whenever I address a group of DP training directors, I always tell a Nate Newkirk story. Nate teaches the BSI course called *How to Implement a DP Human Resource Development Program* (HRD) which is taught every October and May in Washington. Nate is a super guy and has a million stories, so I always swipe this one from him because it sets the proper tone for his course and for my speeches.

Nate found himself with some time to kill one time when he was visiting Atlanta, Georgia. He decided to go to the public library. Nate looked up on a shelf in the history section of the library. There he saw a book whose title will forever be immortalized, if not by its readers, at least by Nate and me.

(The text of a speech presented by Gary Slaughter to a number of fledgling DP training director organizations around the country.)

The book was entitled, *An Unbiased View of the War Between the States, as the South Sees It.*

Today, you're going to hear an unbiased view of how to organize a DP training director's group ... as Gary Slaughter sees it. My first "unbiased" and experienced viewpoint is encompassed by *Slaughter's Irrevocable Law of Adhocracy* which states:

> Voluntary, membership organizations—no matter what kind—will only continue to exist for as long as they continue to produce beneficial services to all of their members.

I don't know why people can't follow this law ... maybe it's against human nature or something. But, I can assure you that you are bound to fail if you don't follow it.

Here are three corollaries for sure failure:

1. Let your organization become an ego trip for a few strong personalities who can't lead at the office or at home, so they come to your training group and take it out on you.
2. Let your organization become myopic and don't open your minds to all points of view.
3. Let your organization become a "playground" for vendors. Beware of vendors! They seduce you with promises of objectivity, then "sell" with a vengeance, just when you get dependent upon them.

Obviously, BSI should be the only vendor, you should let talk to you at all. Seriously, we are no exception. Give us an "inch" and we'll sell it back to you as a "mile."

Today, there are DP training directors groups in the following cities, at least groups that I know about which are functioning: New York, Chicago, Pittsburgh, Detroit, Philadelphia, Omaha, Hartford, Boston, Toronto, Minneapolis, Denver, and Toledo. Three of these groups are about to go the way of the Roman Empire ... down and out (of existence, that is). The reason—they have stopped providing beneficial services to *all* of their members.

I'd like to tell you about some services that you should consider. These are services that I have seen work and work well ... for groups all over the country. I'd also like to tell you about some services, or disservices, that I've seen work poorly so you don't make the same mistake.

Before I discuss services, it's important for you to know how some of these DP training directors groups are organized, so let's spend time going over some of the choices you have in these four "organizational" areas: membership and attendance, organizational structure, affiliations, and finances. Incidentally, I don't know if you have a constitution or charter yet, but these aspects should be made a part of your charter.

I think the best way to acquaint you with your organizational "choices" is to review how some of the more successful groups around the country are organized. I'll be talking about some pretty large, formal groups. Don't be intimidated. Simply pick and choose from those characteristics that fit your group comfortably.

Let's look first at *Chicago*. The Chicago group is called CDPEC which stands for Chicago D.P. Education Council. I'll talk about this group in great detail because I consider it to be the most successful. This organization is characterized by its membership limitations and strict rules relating to attendance, financial obligations, and so on. Chicago is a big DP city, and I'm not sure that many other cities could support organizations which are as "clubbish" as CDPEC and get away with it.

CDPEC limits its members to:

1. *Large DP* users who operate in the Chicago area, have at least one full-time DP trainer, and who are relatively large IBM users (i.e., have a 350/145 or larger).

2. *Prospective members* must submit rather elaborate membership petitions which include the following information:

    a. DP department organization chart

    b. Specific educational objectives and schedule of courses for the upcoming period (i.e., you must already be in the DP training business to join)

    c. Configuration description

    d. Written statement from the DP manager stating the corporate commitment to DP training and specific plans for and resources for meeting that commitment

    e. Description of the corporate (or DP) training philosophy—i.e., why you do it and why we do what we do.

These limitations and restrictions on membership are understandable when you look at the size of some of the founding CDPEC members such as International Harvester, Kraft, Sears Roebuck, Standard Oil of Indiana, Time, Inc., and so on. Each of the organizations have two to three DP trainers in each of several divisions. These people have taken the selfish but understandable attitude that they don't want to waste their time with the little guy's problems. Your members may have a different attitude.

CDPEC's new members must be approved by a two-thirds vote of all members with each company having one vote. CDPEC meets monthly on the second Thursday at 9:00 a.m. The meeting format is:

Business meeting first—various routine topics, special reports, etc.

Formal presentations from someone selected by the program committee

Followed by luncheon—paid for by the members individually

These meetings are held by host companies on a rotating basis, in classrooms or meeting rooms, at the host company site. In the case of CDPEC, members are spread from Waugegan to Gary which must be 60 miles or more. I feel strongly about the value of seeing how the other person lives, i.e., having meetings at each member's offices. Part of the meeting, incidentally, is devoted to a brief overview of the host's configuration, people organization, and training function.

The CDPEC program committee is very important. This committee is made up of three members who serve for nine months each. Each three months a new committee member is added to the program committee. The member who has been there for six months, assumes the chairpersonship of the committee. This person also chairs the general sessions and coordinates the various adhoc working groups dividing the three-month reign. I really like this approach. It keeps a fresh group of ideas pouring into the program, it provides for some continuity, and it spreads the work around in an equitable fashion.

CDPEC is a very democratic organization. There are no officers, just the program committee. There is a membership committee, but that's all in the way of formalization.

CDPEC is very strict about participation and attendance. Each company must send a representative to each meeting. They have a problem with too many people attending usually, so they limit attendance to 2 people per company, unless you have multiple DP training groups, then it's one person per unit. They want the same individual to attend, if at all possible, for continuity's sake. If you miss two consecutive meetings you are notified that you are "irregular" in attendance. At the third meeting, if you're not there, you lose your CDPEC membership. In addition to these formal constitutional rules, CDPEC has issued several policy statements that are, in effect, constitutional amendments. These are:

1. Nonaggression hiring agreement—If you share a CONSORTIUM training session with another member company, you can't pirate that company's employees from them (particularly important with the high turnover of today).

2. Tuition subscription guarantee—If you commit to support a CDPEC CONSORTIUM by reserving seats, then cancel after 15 days before the course, you're obligated to pay for the course seats anyway. This rule helps organize Chicago CONSORTIUMS. We've had three successful SAW CONSORTIUMS there so far, so the policy must work well.

3. Attendance and lunch guarantee—If you say you're coming to lunch, you must pay, even if you don't show up.

4. Guest policy—Prospective members may observe CDPEC meetings for a period of three consecutive meetings only. By the fourth meeting, the prospective member must petition to join CDPEC.

Here's a free Slaughter editorial comment, another unbiased opinion: The exclusiveness of the CDPEC "club" has soured some people on joining CDPEC. These are usually the one-person training organizations who don't want to be committed to attend every meeting and so on. However, in general, by the looks of its active membership, I judge that the exclusiveness draws envy from outsiders. In fact, I know one DP training director who couldn't get his boss to sign the letter of commitment required in the new membership petition, so he said that's it and put out his resume.

Let's talk about *Pittsburgh*—The SIG/EDP of ASTD. Mr. Pittsburgh DP Training is John Rose. In fact, John may be Mr. DP Training for the entire country. John has been in DP training for years, since the 1950s.

As the senior Pittsburgh DP trainer, John, because of an elaborate justification that any member of the Pittsburgh group will send to you in one of their "rainbow packs," decided that this group should affiliate with ASTD, the American Society for Training & Development.

I support, strongly, individual ASTD membership and attendance of the ASTD National Conference. My reason for advocating ASTD membership for DP Training Directors is simply that DP trainers generally know much more about DP than they do about training, and I would like to see DP training people do a more professional job, so they are around after our next economic downturn. I lost too many DP training friends after the 1971 and 1975 downturns to make me feel comfortable.

Let's get back to the Pittsburgh group. The Pittsburgh group is organized differently than the Chicago group. They have officers and several standing committees like most formal organizations have. They also have a recruitment problem ... or at least a desire to grow. They currently have 22 companies ranging in size from very large, like Westinghouse, to small, like Allegheny County Government. Mind you, John is still a strong influence, but not so much in the limelight ... he's merely treasurer.

Pittsburgh has done something that I think is great. Each member company that joins the organization must contribute $1,000 to a common pool. An account is established for every organization which is started with the initial contribution and goes up and down with exchange of training services among members. This system was established to enable organizations to exchange services on an equitable and fair basis. The group established an arbitrary but fair fee of $85 per student day for all training offered to other members of the group. If Company A's student attends Company B's one-day course, Company A's account is debited $85 and Company B's account is credited $85. If you draw your account down to zero dollars, you must contribute another $1,000.

The need for this accounting system also stems from the shrewd business deal that John Rose negotiated with Edutronics a few years ago, a deal that made Pittsburgh a non-ASI and non-Deltak town especially as far as small users were concerned. John negotiated a contract with Edutronics to establish a complete Edutronics library at PPG Industries, John's company, and to allow any SIG/EDP member to draw films out of that library and pay only the standard, one-time charge for this film. Each company using Edutronics' films in this way shifts funds from its account to the PPG account. PPG is responsible for paying Edutronics.

Incidentally, I was in Pittsburgh in November 1978, speaking before the SIG/EDP group on cost justifying training. The Edutronics representative was there and asserted that other cities could still negotiate this same deal with Edutronics. ASI and Deltak won't touch it with a 10-foot pole.

By the way, because John set up this elaborate accounting system is probably the reason he's still treasurer.

I'll mention CONSORTIUM training later, but the Pittsburgh group has used this method of charging their members for participation in two very successful CONSORTIUM offerings held earlier this year.

Finally, the Pittsburgh group meets for formal meetings, one Friday per month. They meet informally for lunch each Friday for a "brown bag" theater. Here they review a new film or two and chat about training problems over a bag lunch. This is accommodated by the close proximity of members to each other. Almost all members are within a five-minute walk of PPG Industries which is right at the apex of Pittsburgh's Golden Triangle area.

Let's take a look at the New York group, called TIME. TIME stands for "Trainers Involved in Media Education." TIME is now involved in all kinds of DP training. Incidentally, I recommend not restricting yourself to any one training medium. TIME was initially established as an ASI-sponsored ASI users group. Over a period of time, the group withdrew from that sponsorship relationship with ASI ... that was not an easy withdrawal from what I understand.

The TIME group does an interesting thing each year. As a group, they ask each member to provide detailed comments on the products and services of the three principal A-V vendors. TIME then forwards the comments and criticism to these vendors with an invitation to come before the group to defent themselves—at separate meetings, naturally.

A number of contractual and service inconsistencies have been uncovered through this process, so they repeat it every year. It's amazing what you learn when you compare notes. That's why at BSI we have one published price list so that everybody is charged the same thing for BSI services.

Let's look at Philadelphia. Philadelphia is blessed with two DP training groups. One is an ASI users group called D-VUE and the other is a DELTAK users group called VU-POINT. I am more familiar with vu-point, because I spoke before that group. They have established a very workable—at least it appears that way—arm's length relationship with DELTAK, a relationship that appears to benefit both sides.

I might digress a moment to give you my unbiased opinion on affiliating with a vendor. My opinion is—stay clear of it. As a vendor, I know that I would not want to foot your printing and mailing bills, meeting room charges, lunches, and cocktails unless I exerted considerable control over your group. If you don't mind this sometimes, not-so-subtle manipulation, censorship, and restriction, go ahead and affiliate with one of the A-V vendors; any of the three would be happy to have you as a users group. You'll notice I said A-V vendors—don't ask BSI to sponsor you. I would not want to compromise your success by exerting—what to me would be—necessary control over you.

I said initially that we would talk about service to membership. How can you keep your members happy?

1. Maintain an active program of outside "experts." Don't get inbred. Allow time to talk and compare notes with each

other, but look for outside stimulation for your programs even if you have to pay.

2. Organize to be financially independent, so you can pay for your programs. Also, offer programs to your community. Cooperate with other local DP professional groups like DPMA. Cosponsor programs and charge people to attend ... build a fund for even better programs.

3. Sponsor training courses in the CONSORTIUM format. Survey your members' needs and offer courses that fit those needs.

If you can't get the other vendors to work with you, contact me. We are delighted to help DP training directors' organizations succeed using CONSORTIUM training. We have had successful CONSORTIUM training offerings through every major DP training directors group in the country. We'd like to help you here as well.

Our CONSORTIUM sponsors can attest to the kind of support we give them in the form of our CONSORTIUM Sponsor's Guide, mailing lists, and invoicing services, if need be. We would be happy to prorate the cost of any of our standard in-house courses across the course attendees, invoice, and collect each organization's share. We try to take the hassle out of DP trainers groups' sponsoring CONSORTIUM training.

Is everyone familiar with the economics of CONSORTIUM training? BSI charges eight times the standard public course fee to conduct a standard course in the CONSORTIUM format for up to 25 students. You get a top-notch BSI training course and a first-string instructor for a fraction of the cost of a public course in Washington or New York, and you avoid all the travel expense.

4. Share competitive knowledge. Establish a list of common problems facing members. Form committees to solve these problems and to share the results. Publish the results. Offer them to other DP training groups. Send them to me to publish in the *BSI Insider News*.

5. Present a united buyer's front to DP training vendors. Bargain for special deals such as the Pittsburgh group bargained for. Exert pressure on non-cooperative vendors. Try these pressure tactics with all the BSI competitors, please.

6. Put the spotlight on your members. When someone does something special, give him or her the kind of credit that gets back to their boss. Give recognition. Pat each other on the back. Build credibility for each other. All DP trainers can use it!

Above all, involve your DP managers in this group. Do things for them. Get them interested in making sure your group survives and succeeds.

7. Have fun. Have your meetings in interesting places. Show films, entertain, and amuse your members, if not educate them. In short, don't take yourselves too seriously.

8. The last tip is, promote professionalism. Do everything you can do as an organization to make DP training the kind of profession that we all can be proud of.

I'd like to come back here some day to talk to you again. When I do, I'd like you to still be here.

Thank you.

BIBLIOGRAPHY

Becker, Stephen P. "How to prove-and-report Return on (Training) Investment." *Training HRD*, May 1978, pp. 39–40.

Brandon Systems Institute, *1977–78 Annual DP Training Survey*. Bethesda: Brandon Systems Institute, 1978.

Brudner, Harvey J. "Gedanken Experiments in Educational Cost Effectiveness." *Technical Horizons in Education Journal*, 1978, pp. 31–37.

Bunker, Kerry A., and Cohen, Stephen L. "Evaluating organizational training efforts: Is ignorance really bliss?" *Training and Development Journal*, August 1978, pp. 4–11.

Cantwell, John A. "Benefits of In-House Continuing Education for Knowledge Workers." *National Report for Training and Development*, 1977, p. 2.

Comstock, Steven H. *An Analysis of Alternatives in Data Processing Training*. Denver: Unpublished Manuscript, 1978.

Connors, J. "1976–Looking Ahead." *Training and Development Journal*, January 1976, pp. 28–31.

"Cost-Justification of In-House Training." A paper prepared by the Cost-Justification Project, Training and Education Group, Guide International, August 1978.

Craig, Robert L., *Training and Development Handbook*. New York: McGraw-Hill, 1976.

Cullen, James G.; Sawzin, Stephen A.; Sisson, Gary R.; Swanson, Richard A. "Cost Effectiveness: A Model for Assessing the Training Investment." *Training and Development Journal*, January 1978, pp. 24–30.

Cullen, James G.; Sawzin, Steven A.; Sisson, Gary R.; Swanson, Richard A. "Training, What's It Worth?" *Training and Development Journal*, August 1976, pp. 12–20.

DeCotiis, Thomas A., and Morano, Richard A. "Applying job analysis to training." *Training and Development Journal*, July 1977, pp. 20–24.

Deltak Productivity Breakfast. Notes from meeting, Chicago, April 19, 1978.

Deterline, William A. "Credibility in Training" (a series of six articles). *Training and Development Journal*, December 1976–June 1977, pp. var.

Drucker, Peter. "Interview." *Training HRD*, October 1977, pp. var.

Elsbree, Asia Rial, and Howe, Christine. "An evaluation of training in three acts" (three-part article). *Training and Development Journal*, July 1977–September 1977, pp. var.

Forest, Robert B. "What are we measuring?" *Infosystems*, May 1978, pp. 92–94.

Fram, Eugene H. "What to Do Before and After Budget Cuts!" *Training and Development Journal*, January 1978, pp. 40–45.

Gilbert, Thomas F. "Training: The $100 Billion Opportunity." *Training and Development Journal*, November 1976, pp 3–8.

Hahne, C.E. "How to measure the results of sales training." *Training and Development Journal*, November 1977, pp. var.

Hopper, Grace. An address before the Deltak Users Conference, Chicago, April 19, 1978.

Kirkpatrick, Donald L., compiler. *Evaluating Training Programs*. Madison: American Society for Training and Development, 1975.

———. "Evaluating Training Programs: Evidence vs. Proof." *Training and Development Journal*, November 1977, pp. 31–33.

———. "Techniques for evaluating training programs" (four-part article). *Training and Development Journal*, 1978, pp. var.

Konczal, Edward F. "Planning for Training at AT&T." *Training and Development Journal*, April 1978, pp. 3–8.

Laird, Dugan. "Is your training staff delivering payoff? Score yourself and them with this quiz." *Training HRD*, October 1977, p. 94.

McCullough, Richard C. "Trainer, Train Thyself for Tight Times." *The Torch*, May 1976, p. 1.

Matthews, Bonnye L. "Training More Employees for Less Money." *Training and Development Journal*, September 1978, pp. 44–50.

Mirabal, Thomas E. "Forecasting Future Training Costs." *Training and Development Journal*, July 1978, pp. 78–88.

Newkirk, Nate A., course developer. *Cost Benefit Analysis for DP Systems (CBA)* (two-day training course). Bethesda: Brandon Systems Institute, 1978.

———. "Evaluating Training Results—Theory and Practice." *BSI Insider News*, Spring 1978, pp. 1–2.

———. course developer. *How to Implement a DP Human Resource Development Program (HRD)* (five-day training course). Bethesda: Brandon Systems Institute, 1978.

———. "Justifying the Training Budget." *BSI Insider News*, Winter 1978, pp. 1–2.

Oliver, Paul. "Examining Programming Costs." *Computer Decisions*, April 1978, pp. 50–52.

Palaniappan, Pl. "A healthy look at return on investment." *Infosystems*, February 1978, pp. 99–100.

Peeples, Donald E. "Measure for Productivity." *Datamation*, May 1978, pp. 222–230.

Ricks, Don M. "The day the boss learned how expensive 'cheap' training can be." *Training HRD*, June 1978, pp. 50, 52–53.

Rummler, Geary A. "You need performance, not training." *Training HRD*, October 1977, pp. var.

Scherer, W. T. "How to Get Management's Commitment for Training." *Training and Development Journal*, January 1978, pp. 3–8.

Scott, Ralph K. "Management's dilemma: to train or not to train people." *Training and Development Journal*, February 1978, pp 3–6.

"Solidify your training budget ... tell management how good a job you're doing." *BSI Insider News*, Spring 1978, pp. 5–6.

"Study shows verbal praise increases performance." *Government Training News*, March 1978, p. 6.

Toellner, John. "Performance Measurement in Systems and Programming" (two-part article). *Infosystems*, December 1977 and January 1978, pp. 34–36 and pp. 60–62.

Ware, Robert B. "Follow up, alternatives and rewards: Three pillars of cost effective training." *Infosystems*, March 1978, pp. 98–99.

———. "Precision Planning: The basic foundation of cost-effective training." *Infosystems*, January 1978, p. 64.

———. "Training: Why does it cost so much?" *Infosystems*, February 1977, p. 107.

Zemke, Ron. "Management training and development: Measuring the impact ... " *Training HRD*, October 1977, pp. 62–64.

INDEX